Critical Thinking in Consumer Behavior

Cases and Experiential Exercises

Critical Thinking in Consumer Behavior

Cases and Experiential Exercises
Second Edition

Judy Graham, Ph.D.
Saint John Fisher College

Prentice Hall

Boston   Columbus   Indianapolis   New York   San Francisco   Upper Saddle River

Amsterdam   Cape Town   Dubai   London   Madrid   Milan   Munich   Paris   Montreal   Toronto

Delhi   Mexico City   Sao Paulo   Sydney   Hong Kong   Seoul   Singapore   Taipei   Tokyo

Editor-in-Chief: Eric Svendsen
Acquisitions Editor: James Heine
Editorial Project Manager: Ashley Santora
Production Project Manager: Debbie Ryan
Operations Specialist: Arnold Vila

Prentice Hall
is an imprint of

www.pearsonhighered.com

16 2020

ISBN-13: 978-0-13-602716-4
ISBN-10: 0-13-602716-4

TABLE OF CONTENTS

Foreword   *iv*
   by David Bakken, Ph.D.

Preface   *v*

SECTION I: The Importance of Customer Centricity   **1**

   1. Customer Retention and Profitability   3
   2. Measuring Customer Loyalty with the Net Promoter Score™   4
   3. Customer Experience Management   9

SECTION II: Customer Perception   **23**

   4. Information Overload   25
   5. The Just Noticeable Difference   27
   6. Perceptual Maps   29

SECTION III: Customer Learning and Memory   **37**

   7. Behavioral Learning: Classical and Operant Conditioning   39
   8. Memorable Taglines   44
   9. Memory Models and Promotional Strategies   49

SECTION IV: Customer Motivation and Personality   **55**

   10. The Great Debate   57
   11. Maslow's Need Hierarchy and Customer Motivation   61
   12. Appealing to the Id, Superego, and Ego   65

SECTION V: Segmenting, Targeting, and Positioning   **67**

   13. VALS™ Segmentation Categories   69
   14. Positioning Strategies   74
   15. Adopter Categories   76

SECTION VI: Reference Group Influence and Diffusion of Innovation   **81**

   16. Forms of Reference Group Influence   83
   17. Types of Reference Groups   87
   18. Diffusion of Innovation   89

SECTION VII: Customer Attitudes   **91**

    19. Hierarchies of Effects   93
    20. The Fishbein Model of Attitude Measurement   97
    21. The Extended Fishbein Model   100

SECTION VIII: Marketing Communication and Attitude Change   **105**

    22. Multiattribute Models and Attitude Change Strategies   107
    23. The Elaboration Likelihood Model   110
    24. Social Judgment Theory and Attitude Change   113
    25. Balance Theory and Spokesperson Strategies   116

SECTION IX: Customer Decision Making   **123**

    26. Group/Family Decision Making   125
    27. Decision Heuristics   127
    28. Decision Rules I: Introduction to Decision Rules   132
    29. Decision Rules II: The Application of Decision Rules   137

SECTION X: Qualitative and Interpretive Consumer Research   **139**

    30. Projective Techniques   141
    31. Laddering Interviews and Means-End Analysis   146
    32. Information Display Boards   152

SECTION XI: Cultural and Subcultural Influences   **157**

    33. The Diversity of Customer Behavior   159
    34. Culture and Customer Behavior   160
    35. The Chinese Consumer   164

<u>Dedication</u>

This book is dedicated to:

My husband, Mark, who has been sharing his steadfast love and good humor with me for over a quarter of a century. I can't imagine a happier life than the one we've built together.

My children, Meghan, Kelsey, and Laura, whose love, laughter, wisdom, and great generosity of spirit make my world magical.

My parents, Ron and Doris Frazer, who showed me the way.

Foreword

While I was a graduate student in psychology, I took sailing lessons offered by the excellent community boating program run by the Metropolitan District Commission in Boston. I learned to tie a bowline knot—important to sailors—using a mnemonic device involving a rabbit emerging from its hole and running around a tree. I can still tie a bowline knot. However, it's been many years since I took the lessons, and I can no longer remember *why* I would want to tie a bowline. I cannot remember the purpose of a bowline because I have not needed one since I stopped sailing.

We learn many things in the classroom and from textbooks, but until we apply that learning to action, we have not really acquired *knowledge*. These case studies offer you, the student of consumer behavior, the opportunity to apply the concepts you've acquired through readings and lectures. A number of years ago, I taught, on a part-time basis, an upper level course in consumer behavior. In my experience, one of the greatest challenges of this course lies in getting students to see the connection between a principle or theory covered in the classroom and real-life consumer marketing problems that are not covered specifically in the text or lectures. The cases in this book provide you with opportunities to practice using the theories of consumer behavior in solving realistic marketing problems.

Some of the cases are straightforward exercises that will reinforce the course concepts. The exercises on classical and instrumental conditioning, for example, provide several real-world examples that will help students recognize the use of learning theory in marketing campaigns. The many extended cases also give students models for the application of consumer psychology in the "real world" inhabited by marketing managers, product managers, and marketing research practitioners.

I have been involved in the practice of consumer research for over 20 years, and I am very impressed with these cases and their capacity to help students internalize the concepts of consumer behavior. Even students who do not pursue careers in marketing will become better-informed decision makers as a result of completing these cases and exercises. Since many of you who do pursue careers in marketing will be drawn to careers in marketing research, your ability to apply what you've learned about consumer behavior to specific client problems will be very valuable to both your employers and your clients.

David G. Bakken, Ph.D.
Senior Vice President
Strategic Research Solutions
Harris Interactive Inc.

Preface

An understanding of the customer is now widely recognized as a necessary component to business success in the 21st century. In the business world, the importance of what is known as "customer centricity" cannot be overstated. The world's best companies rely on customer metrics as indicators of business success throughout the enterprise, as well as vital dimensions of employees' performance evaluations. These same companies assess prospective employees on customer centricity criteria as they apply for a job. Customer centricity has become, in effect, a crucial doctrine in the world of business. And more than any other course in a business curriculum, a course in consumer behavior offers this essential knowledge.

In the study of business, most learning objectives involve the attainment of two types of knowledge: understanding and competency. An *understanding* of the concepts and theories of consumer behavior is typically attained through the textbook and other assigned readings, as well as classroom discussions. *Competency* with these concepts, or the ability to effectively use and apply these concepts to unfamiliar situations, is usually more difficult for students to attain. The cases and exercises included in this book are designed to give students opportunities to critically analyze important concepts related to consumer behavior, and gain competency in their application within the complexities of the business world.

The level of difficulty of the cases and exercises varies widely. Some of them are very easy to complete, yet provide an enduring and unforgettable lesson. Others pose more of a challenge. As you complete these cases and exercises, there will be many times when you feel confident in your ability to apply the consumer behavior concepts you are learning to the task at hand, and there will be other times when it seems that you could not possibly have enough knowledge to complete the task successfully. Although you may sometimes feel that you are being "thrown to the wolves," remember that it is when the wolves are nipping at your heels that you discover how fast you can run. As you are working on those cases that seem particularly challenging, remember to review the relevant concepts in your class notes and textbook, then trust your creativity and resourcefulness—this is what great businesspeople are made of.

Lastly, have some fun with the cases. The study of consumer behavior is not quite like the study of any other topic in business. Enjoy these opportunities to become truly customer centric. Just as customer centricity is essential to an organization's success, it is also essential to your future business success.

Acknowledgments

I wish to thank those who have helped make this book possible. My team at Pearson Prentice Hall, Melissa (Pellerano) Gill, Ashley Santora, and James Heine, were a joy to work with. The reviewers of the first edition of this text, especially Mike Solomon and David Bakken, offered valuable comments and encouragement. My colleagues at St. John Fisher College cheered on my progress and provided inspiration through their dedication to teaching. My family and friends gave me their unwavering love through the ups and downs of the creative process. Thank you.

About the Author

Judy F. Graham, Ph.D., is a Professor at St. John Fisher College in Rochester, New York, where she teaches undergraduate and MBA courses in Marketing and Customer Behavior. Prior to obtaining her Ph.D. in Business Administration/Marketing from Syracuse University, she worked with AT&T Corporation and was one of the youngest employees in the organization to receive a promotion to senior national account executive. She has published her scholarly research in such journals as the *Journal of Marketing Theory and Practice, Psychology and Marketing*, and the *Journal of Social Behavior and Personality*. Her current research interests involve social marketing campaigns and gender differences in customer information processing. She has been a visiting professor in Europe and most recently for China Europe International Business School's (CEIBS) MBA program (ranked 11th globally, *Financial Times*, 2008) in Shanghai, China. Professor Graham and her husband, Mark, have three grown children. She and her family love to travel, and they have visited 18 countries and nearly every U.S. National Park.

SECTION I:

THE IMPORTANCE OF CUSTOMER CENTRICITY

1. Customer Retention and Profitability

Pete Palermo is owner and proprietor of Pete's Pizza Parlor, a restaurant that specializes in pizza, wings, and submarine sandwiches. The business is mostly take-out, although there are a few booths available for those customers who want to dine in. Pete has been in business for over 10 years, and his business is well established in an upper-middle-class suburb of a Northeastern U.S. city.

Pete's annual revenues are strong—he typically sees $350,000 in sales per year. His various costs, including a salary for both him and his wife, who works at the restaurant and serves as bookkeeper, have also been high, and he normally sees about 5% profits—$17,500 this past year.

Pete is taking some courses in business at the local college. One of his classes is in marketing, and he's been hearing a lot about the importance of customer satisfaction and retention. His professor has said that it is typically 5–10 times more expensive to attract a new customer than it is to keep a current customer. And on television recently, he heard world business leaders say that if you can retain 5% more of your customers than you currently do, your bottom-line profit will grow between 25% and 50%. All of this has caught Pete's interest, and he's been doing some research on the subject in the college's library.

He's learned that in his type of business, maintaining a current patron runs about $20 per year, while attracting a new customer is six times higher—$120. He's also learned that of those customers who stop patronizing a business, about two-thirds of them do so because of discourteous treatment they've received at that business, whereas less than 15% do so because of product quality.

Pete's been thinking a lot about this. Ever since he's opened the business, he's been a stickler for using the very best ingredients and freshest toppings on his pizzas. He has thought very little about the type of treatment that his customers receive—it has always seemed to him that if the pizza is good the customers will come back. But he knows that this clearly isn't the case. He serves about 1,200 suburban families in his area, and he feels that this is a comfortable customer base for his business. His retention rate per year is about 75%. In other words 25%, or 300 families, choose to stop using his restaurant in any given year, and he must replace those lost customers with 300 new ones. His retention rate is not bad for his type of business, but now Pete is wondering if he might, with some very small changes in the ways that his employees deal with patrons, be able to increase his retention rates.

Please answer the following:

1. If Pete's customer base remains at 1,200 and he increases his customer retention rate by 5%, what increase in profits will Pete see? (Please state your answer in a dollar amount.)

2. Given that Pete's most recent profits were $17,500, what *percentage increase* in profits does your answer to question 1 represent?

2. Measuring Customer Loyalty with the Net Promoter Score™

Six months ago, Alexander opened a new branch office of his company, Ty-D-Home, in San Francisco. The San Francisco office is his sixth office—he already had three offices in Los Angeles and two in San Diego. His business provides home cleaning services for busy working people and families. The cleaning industry is booming, and Alexander's customer base has been steadily climbing. However, even with the growth in absolute customer numbers that Alexander has been experiencing, he knows that his market share is dwindling. In other words, his competitors are growing at a pace faster than his. Alexander's sense is that this is due to their higher customer retention rates. Since the industry as a whole is growing, both he and his competitors are acquiring new customers at a steady rate, but because his competitors are better able to hold on to their customers, their growth is outpacing his.

Whereas it is tempting for Alexander to focus on his steadily climbing customer numbers and ignore his dwindling market share and low customer retention rates, he knows that this would be devastating to his future success. Like all business owners, he understands that customer retention is crucial to profitability. He also realizes that low customer retention rates are a signal that things are not going as well in his business as he would like them to be.

Alexander knows he needs to address this problem head-on. Why is he losing customers? Who is he losing, and why?

For the past few years, Alexander has belonged to a business owners group that convenes once a quarter. The members also keep in touch on the group's website by posting questions and joining discussion threads. Alexander has always seen this group as an important resource, so he logged on to the site and searched phrases like "customer retention" and "customer loyalty." What he found astounded him. A term that he had never seen before was popping up everywhere: NPS, or Net Promoter Score.[1]

As Alexander further researched NPS, he learned that the basic idea behind it was to ask current customers whether they would recommend your product or service to someone else. At first, Alexander thought that he was misunderstanding the explanation. Whereas word of mouth is very important to his business, at the moment he was not looking for a way to track word of mouth—he was interested in exploring customer loyalty issues! Digging a little deeper into the issue, he found out why there was so much excitement surrounding this seemingly simple customer inquiry: Many of his peers believed that a customer's "willingness to recommend" is the *one best indicator* of that customer's future loyalty. The reasoning is this: If customers are willing to recommend a product/service to others, they are putting their own reputation on the line, and they are only willing to do that if they are very satisfied with, and hence will be very loyal to, that product/service.

How had he missed this? When did everyone go from talking about customer satisfaction measurements to talking about this NPS? Apparently, many of the business owners he knew

---

[1] Net Promoter, NPS, and Net Promoter Score are trademarks of Satmatrix Systems, Inc., Bain & Company, and Fred Reichheld.

were already tying their employees' bonuses and other compensation to Net Promoter Scores. He was feeling incredibly out of the loop on this one, and began researching the issue in earnest.

Alexander's research led him to a large number of articles, including a *BusinessWeek* article[2] that Alexander was surprised he had missed. Eventually his search led him to what he was looking for: the 2003 *Harvard Business Review* article that was the foundation of this movement: "The One Number You Need to Grow," by Frederick Reichheld.[3] He learned that by asking his customers to answer just one question, he could classify each responding customer as a "Promoter"; a "Passively Satisfied"; or a "Detractor," and that his business's Net Promoter Score could be established by subtracting the percentage of Detractors from the percentage of Promoters.

So now Alexander understood how to establish his Net Promoter Score, but he realized that the score meant very little unless he was able to compare his NPS to businesses that were similar to his. After all, one of the reasons he started this process was due to his shrinking market share—he wanted to know how his NPS stacked up against others in his industry. He redirected his search to a website for an industry association group that he belonged to, and began a search for Net Promoter Score. He quickly found his answer in a recent issue of the association's trade journal. Of the businesses that had already conducted NPS reviews, it looked like the average was running around 25. Alexander was certain he could beat that.

As Alexander spent more time researching the NPS process, he found that once the overall NPS is calculated for his business as a whole and then evaluated relative to industry norms, more specific NPS calculations should be done on the data that has been collected. These more specific Net Promoter Scores could be calculated based on particular customer groups, service providers, branch offices, etc., and then be used to illuminate patterns of high and low customer loyalty across different market segments and different parts of the business.

In addition, he should use each customer's initial classification to guide plans for follow-up research regarding each of the specific groups of respondents. For instance, he could engage "Detractors" with research specifically designed to uncover the root causes of their dissatisfaction, while simultaneously using other research methods to explore the best practices that might underlie the responses of the "Promoters."

The concept of tracking customer opinion was not new to Alexander. Twice in the last decade he had hired research firms to conduct customer satisfaction surveys for him. In both cases, the resulting data had been of little real use to him. Both firms had created a very lengthy customer questionnaire, and as a result the customer response rates had been dismal. The responses that did come back provided very little insight. Most customers just went down all the traditional items involving specific service issues and ticked off 4 on the traditional 1–5 customer service scales; it was as if they were just trying to get it over with. And almost no one provided comments in the open-ended section of the questionnaire. Looking back, Alexander felt that he had spent a lot of money for no real benefit.

---

[2] McGregor, J. (2006, January 30). "Would You Recommend Us?" *BusinessWeek*, pp. 94–95.
[3] Reichheld, F. (2003). "The One Number You Need to Grow," *Harvard Business Review*.

As Alexander thought about the possibility of gathering information related to his own Net Promoter Score, he was very attracted to the simplicity of the NPS approach. This seemed to be something that he could do without the help of an outside market research firm. He had long ago established a very basic customer database, and he wondered if he could use that database information along with the NPS approach to begin to answer questions related to Ty-D-Home's customer retention problems. He went back to re-read the original *Harvard Business Review* article by Reichheld, and was pleased to find a complete "How-To" section embedded in that article. This "How-To" section, called "A Net Promoter Primer," is excerpted below:

A Net Promoter Primer:

Firms with the highest net promoter scores consistently garner the lion's share of industry growth. So how can companies get started?

Survey a statistically valid sample of your customers with the following question: "How likely is it that you would recommend [brand or company X] to a friend or colleague?" It's critical to provide a consistent scale for responses that range from zero to ten, where zero means not at all likely, five means neutral, and ten means extremely likely.

Resist the urge to let survey questions diminish response rates along with the reliability of your sample. You need only one question to determine the status—promoter, passively satisfied, or detractor—of a customer. (Follow-up questions can help unearth the reasons for customers' feelings and point to profitable remedies. But such questions should be tailored to the three categories of customers. Learning how to turn a passively satisfied customer into a promoter requires a very different line of questioning from learning how to resolve the problems of a detractor.)

Calculate the percentage of customers who respond with nine or ten (promoters) and the percentage who respond with zero through six (detractors). Subtract the percentage of detractors from the percentage of promoters to arrive at your net promoter score. Don't be surprised if your score is lower than you expect. The median net promoter score of more than 400 companies in 28 industries (based on some 130,000 customer survey responses gathered over the past two-plus years by Satmetrix, a maker of software for managing real-time customer feedback) was just 16.

Compare net promoter scores from specific regions, branches, service or sales reps, and customer segments. This often reveals root causes of differences as well as best practices that can be shared. What (also) counts, of course, is how your company compares with direct competitors. (Also) have your market researchers survey your competitors' customers using the same method. You can then determine how your company stacks up within your industry and whether your current net promoter number is a competitive asset or a liability.

Improve your score. The companies with the most enthusiastic customer referrals, including eBay, Amazon, and USAA, receive net promoter scores of 75% to more than 80%. For companies aiming to garner world-class loyalty—and the growth and profitability that comes with it—this should be the target.

Ty-D-Home currently has around 2,200 customers spread throughout the six branch offices. Each of the six branch offices employs between 14 and 18 individual house cleaners, and each of these cleaners has approximately 22–25 regular clients. One of each of the six branch office's house cleaners also serves as that branch's office manager, and this person typically has about half the number of regular clients as the other full-time cleaners.

In Ty-D-Home's customer database, Alexander keeps information pertaining to:
- Customer Name
- Customer Phone Number
- Customer E-mail Address
- Ty-D-Home Branch Office
- Cleaning Service Provider (the house cleaner who regularly cleans for that customer)
- Size of Home (approximate square footage; Ty-D-Home cleans every size home, from small apartments to large mansions)
- Number of Occupants in Home (Ty-D-Home's clients include single people and large extended families, as well as everything in between)
- Frequency of Service (Weekly, Bi-Weekly, Monthly)

Alexander decided he would give the NPS approach a try. As part of an e-mail, he sent the following question to all 2,200 of his customers:

How likely is it that you would recommend Ty-D-Home to a friend or colleague? (on a scale of 1–10, where 0 means not at all likely, and 10 means extremely likely).

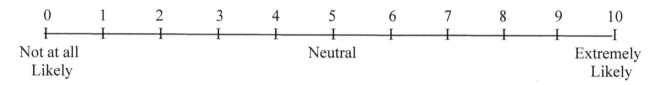

Alexander was pleasantly surprised to get a very high 32% response rate. Here are the results that he received:

0 (not at all likely)......	38
1.........................	10
2.........................	13
3.........................	9
4.........................	16
5 (neutral)...............	72
6.........................	47
7.........................	82
8.........................	100
9.........................	198
10 (extremely likely)....	<u>119</u>
	704 total respondents

Please answer the following questions:

1. What is Ty-D-Home's Net Promoter Score (NPS)?

2. Is this NPS good? Bad? Average?

3. Because Alexander is able to identify each response as a specific customer (by their e-mail address), and so tie that response to the information that he has in his customer database, he is able to perform much more specific analyses beyond the overall NPS (calculated as an answer to question 1). What further *analyses* should Alexander perform on the data he has already collected? Please be specific.

4. What further *follow-up research* (new, more in-depth forms of research) should Alexander undertake with these customers?

5. How might Alexander use the information gleaned from this process to increase his customer retention rates?

3. Customer Experience Management

Customer Experience Management seeks to understand the customer experience from the customer's point of view, and take steps to optimize that experience in a way that maximizes value for both the customer and the organization. Whereas some maintain that Customer Experience Management (CEM) is an integral part of Customer Relationship Management (CRM), others differentiate the two approaches. Meyer and Schwager (2007) note that "CRM captures what a company knows about a particular customer—his or her history of service requests, product returns, and inquiries, among other things—whereas customer experience data capture customers' subjective thoughts about a particular company." These authors further point out that "Although companies know a lot about customers' buying habits, incomes, and other characteristics used to classify them, they know little about the thoughts, emotions, and states of mind that customers' interactions with products, services, and brands induce." (Meyer and Schwager, 2007) A disciplined focus on the thoughts, emotions and states of mind that are induced by customers' interactions with a brand is at the heart of Customer Experience Management.

The Strativity Group has conducted an annual Customer Experience Management Global Survey every year for more than five years. Recent survey results show that whereas 80% of the 379 executives surveyed strongly agreed that customer strategies are now more important to a company's success than ever, their companies still fail to understand their customers' experience in a way that would allow them to design and deliver effective customer strategies. Because of this, they lose customer commitment and loyalty (Strativity Group, 2008). These results illustrate that whereas there is widespread recognition of the power of Customer Experience Management and equally widespread desire to capitalize on its business benefits, many executives appear to be at a loss as to how to realize these benefits.

One of the most powerful means by which companies may realize the benefits of Customer Experience Management involves mapping the customer experience and developing customer strategies based on those maps. Utilizing a customer experience mapping approach involves a number of important steps:

1. Map the customer journey with regard to the brand, including all customer-brand interactions, or "Touch Points."

2. Map that same customer journey as it would look if all interactions were optimal, and compare this new optimal experience map with the customer experience map developed in step 1.

3. Identify company changes that would enhance the customer experience with the brand, and prioritize those changes.

4. Align company employees, processes, policies, and support systems with the changes that have been chosen for implementation.

1. Map the customer journey with regard to the brand, including all customer-brand interactions, or "Touch Points."

David Rickard (2006) proposes that the first step to understanding a customer's experience is to develop a customer life cycle map. He suggests the following as a representative set of typical stages of contact *in an industrial sales context*:

- Relationship Initiation
- Provider Evaluation
- Account Setup
- Order Placement
- Product Reception and Use
- Problem Resolution
- Payment
- Account Maintenance

As part of the creation of this type of map, customer experience investigators must identify the typical stages of a customer's journey with their brand, as well as the typical customer-brand interactions that occur in those stages. In the example above, the first stage of contact in an industrial sales context is termed "Relationship Initiation," and Rickard identifies typical customer-brand interactions within this stage as including interactions such as: "The company exposes the customer to its marketing message" and "The customer seeks relevant information."

The customer life cycle map must be both *comprehensive*, including all potential customer-brand interactions, and *situation-specific*, reflecting the particular realities of a company's business situation. In other words, the above example is merely a generic starting point for those companies marketing in an industrial sales context. Each company must develop a map that identifies the stages of the customer journey and the typical company-brand interactions that exist in their particular business situation.

Meyer and Schwager (2007) point out that companies must be careful to map the complete "customer corridor" of interactions (also known as "touch points") with the company's brands *as well as* with representations of the company's brands. These "representations of the brand" include such things as word of mouth, publicity, customer reviews, blogs, and more.

In many cases, the customer insights that are gleaned from this experience mapping process are a surprise to executives. Most managers begin this process with a very limited understanding of what the customer experience with their brand is like.

2. Map that same customer journey as it would look if all interactions were optimal, and compare this new optimal experience map with the customer experience map developed in step 1.

Once a comprehensive description of the customer journey has been mapped, including typical stages of the customer's journey and all customer-brand interactions particular to each stage, customer experience investigators must then determine what that journey would look like if all interactions were optimal. As is typically the case in marketing strategy endeavors, strategists must identify the optimal market position before measuring how they are performing against it. Therefore, customer experience investigators must develop a clear idea of the experience that they want their customers to have.

This optimal experience map may be difficult to construct. Customer experience investigators must attempt to create a vision of the optimal customer experience that will ultimately drive customer-valued improvements in the company. This requires innovative thinking and necessitates that they "walk in the customer's shoes." An effective way to begin this process is to take each interaction identified in the customer experience map developed in step 1 and brainstorm how that interaction could be modified to be optimally valuable to the customer. Taking the customer's viewpoint is key to this step of the process.

When both the customer experience map and the correlating optimal experience map are in place, customer experience investigators must compare the actual customer experience with the optimal customer experience. They must look for obvious gaps between the two maps, being sure to identify both dissatisfiers (those interactions that leave the customer feeling noticeably disappointed) and opportunities (those interactions that, although not dissatisfying currently, have the potential to delight the customer if optimal customer strategies are put in place).

3. Identify company changes that would enhance the customer experience with the brand, and prioritize those changes.

Customer experience investigators must keep in mind that some touch points, or interactions, are more salient to the customer experience than others. Critical touch points are often referred to as "Moments of Truth." Moments of Truth are those high-impact interactions that have the potential to make or break the total customer experience. Michelle Bottomley, writing for the CRM Project, highlights an airline customer experience mapping project as an example of one company's efforts to understand the customer journey (Bottomley, 2003). By way of example, she notes that for the typical air traveler, the check-in process at the airport can frustrate the air traveler with long lines, thereby making that particular customer-brand interaction very negative. The salient customer frustration makes that part of the customer journey a Moment of Truth. When brainstorming changes that the firm could make to address this, a "drive-through check-in" was identified as a possible modification to that customer-brand interaction, which the customer would experience as optimal.

As part of this process, firms may identify potential internal changes that are fairly straightforward, and that do not require significant modifications to company processes or policies. Many companies are comfortable making these "quick fixes" without further input from customers or further information gathering. In essence, customer experience investigators are choosing to pick off the "low-hanging fruit" first, by making the changes that are easy and that hold promise of improving the total customer experience.

In contrast, other identified internal changes may significantly affect company processes, policies, and/or personnel. Customer experience investigators must prioritize these potential changes, since in most cases companies do not have the resources to make all of the significant changes that have been identified. This means that they must prioritize the identified changes in terms of the feasibility of each change and the degree to which they believe the change will make a significant positive difference in the customer's overall experience with the brand.

There are many means by which marketers prioritize the changes that will produce the "most bang for the buck" in making the customer's experience more positive. Most companies rely heavily on the "voice of the customer" to help them prioritize potential changes. By capturing the voice of the customer, customer experience investigators hope to give top priority to the elements of the customer experience that are the most important to customers. For example, some companies utilize conjoint analysis to analyze the "trade-offs" that customers are willing to make in a customer experience, thereby assessing the relative importance of each facet of the experience to the customer. Companies may also use what is commonly called the "pocketbook" approach. This involves directly asking customers questions such as, "If I were to give you X amount of money, and told you to spend that money making changes to our products/services and the ways in which our company does business, with the stipulation that any monies you spend must be focused on making your customer experience more positive, how much would you spend on each of the different changes?" However a company chooses to infuse the voice of the customer into this prioritization process, it is that voice and a healthy measure of executive judgment that are typically used to prioritize potential changes.

4. Align company employees, processes, policies, and support systems with the changes that have been chosen for implementation.

In many cases, the modifications to processes, policies, and support systems (such as IT systems) that a given change would necessitate will already have been articulated as part of the proposed internal changes identified earlier in this process. But in many cases the important role of employees is overlooked. Company employees play a vital role in the implementation of significant Customer Experience Management changes.

Often, changes related to Customer Experience Management require substantial adjustment to the ways a company motivates its employees and measures their performance. For instance, many companies' call center employees' performance is measured by how quickly they are able to wrap-up an incoming service call. However, if the employees are measured by the speed with which they handle the call, they are likely to attempt to end the call with the customer as quickly as possible, whether or not the customer's issue has been resolved. A focus on the customer experience would encourage the use of a metric such as *first call resolution rates* as a better measure than call center employees' *average call times* when evaluating call center employees' performance. In this example, the first call resolution rate metric aligns employee practices with a focus on the customer experience, whereas the average call time metric typically denigrates the customer experience. Choosing employee incentives and performance measures that are aligned with a focus on the customer experience is an extremely important part of the Customer Experience Management approach.

Because they are so central to the implementation of customer-focused efforts, a company's employees must also be extremely knowledgeable regarding the company's focus on the customer experience. Therefore, educating employees becomes crucial to a company's implementation of customer experience optimization strategies. In addition, because every customer interaction has the potential to be different, front-line employees must also be empowered to implement those customer-focused values in creative and resourceful ways when dealing with high value customers. Hence, customer experience investigators must determine how they will *incent, educate*, and *empower* employees so that they are effectively aligned with the internal changes that have been chosen for implementation.

Scenario:

You have been appointed as part of a cross-functional executive team within CellularStar Corporation, and this team has been tasked with Customer Experience Management (CEM). As part of your initial exploratory work, you have been researching the process of CEM and contacting customers to interview regarding their experiences with CellularStar, a wireless service company serving millions of mobile (cell) phone customers in the United States. Recently, your CEO forwarded to your team a complaint letter (snail mail! who does that anymore?) from a Mr. Harold Sampson addressed to the CEO. There was a very short note from the CEO attached to the letter: "Interview this customer!"

Given little choice in the matter, the team read the letter (the anger and frustration in the letter were palpable) and called Mr. Sampson to offer him generous compensation if he would agree to come to your headquarters and talk with your team about his experiences with CellularStar. You were somewhat surprised when Mr. Sampson agreed to fly in the very next week. He was very gracious over the phone, but given the tone of the letter, you weren't sure what to expect.

When he arrived, you found that he was a personable and courteous man, who asked everyone to call him Hal. He was an operations manager for a company in a small Midwestern city, and assured everyone that he understood the challenges of the business world. Hal recalled everything about his experience with CellularStar with amazing clarity, and the interview ended up lasting over two hours. The team video-recorded the interview and asked questions when appropriate. What follows is Hal's customer journey with CellularStar.

"I was watching TV with my daughter, Rachel, when an ad came on for a type of cell phone that CellularStar has exclusive rights to sell. Rachel loved the commercial, recognized the phone, and said, 'Oh, when I get my cell phone, that's exactly the one I want—it does everything!' Well, her mom and I had been telling her that she couldn't have a cell phone until she turned 14, but lately we had been wondering if it wouldn't be a good idea to get her one sooner than that. She is involved in so much at school—you know how kids are these days—her mom and I had been discussing the value of getting her one when she turned 13—just two months away.

"After Rachel went to bed that evening, I got on the Internet and went to the CellularStar website to see if I could find out more about the phone that Rachel wanted and what it would cost. Well, CellularStar sells a lot of cell phones! I was trying to figure out which cell phone my daughter had seen, but the model in the commercial had a name that was just letters and numbers—something like XJC520 or something—who can remember that? And it seemed like ALL the models on the website had names that were letters and numbers, and they all looked exactly alike to me. Not having any clue where to start, I just started clicking on different models to see if I might be able to figure it out. At that point, I found that I couldn't go anywhere on the site or gather any information about the phones without completing a lengthy registration process. Well, OK, I figured, I would probably be doing business with them sooner or later, given that Rachel wanted a phone that was only sold through them, so I completed the lengthy registration process.

"Once I was 'allowed' on the other pages of CellularStar's site, every time I clicked on one model, I was bumped over to a new web page that was full of an enormous amount of technical information on that model. There didn't appear to be a way to easily compare the basic features of the different models, and I quickly got sick of wading through the reams of information on each model's web page. So I went back to the CellularStar homepage and looked around to see if there was a chat function—I thought maybe if I talked with someone at CellularStar, I might be able to figure it out. However, it didn't look like there was a chat function on the website (although it was hard to tell, because the homepage was so crowded), so I went to the 'contact us' page and decided to e-mail CellularStar a question regarding which phone model had been advertised at the approximate time of night we'd seen the ad on that TV station in my region. I know that was a little strange, but I didn't know how else to ask the question. I've never even bought a cell phone before. Both my wife and I are provided with cell phones through work.

"When I got home from work the next evening, I checked my personal e-mail and there wasn't any response from CellularStar. So I went back to the 'contact us' page and found a number to call. The call was answered very quickly and automatically routed to an IVR (Interactive Voice Response) system. Now, I don't want to be unreasonable here—those things are great money-savers, and we use them at my business too—but there were NO options that fit what I was looking for, and that thing just went on forever. So I hit '0' and was then put on hold for almost 20 minutes. When a human being finally answered, I realized that you had off-shored your call center, and that I was talking to someone thousands of miles away to ask what model of cell phone had been advertised on my local TV station! Needless to say, I thanked the customer service rep and hung up.

"Anyway, while I was on the CellularStar website once again, I tried to find a CellularStar location that was close to our home by looking around the website, but they didn't seem to have the 'store locator' feature, so I looked it up on Yellowpages.com instead. There was a CellularStar location only a few miles away, so I decided to go there after work the next day.

"I got to the CellularStar store the next day and I immediately saw their tagline plastered everywhere, 'Cellular Convenience, Star Service.' Funny, I hadn't seen that tagline on their website—I thought I remembered an entirely different tagline on the website. When I arrived, I checked my watch and saw that it was just 5:30. I was relieved that I had plenty of time to get the phone matter taken care of and meet my wife at our favorite restaurant at 7:00 as planned. I mean the tagline there said that CellularStar stands for Convenience and Service, right? I even started planning the other errands I could get done before I needed to head across town to dinner.

"Immediately inside the door of the store was an old-fashioned sign-up sheet, and there didn't appear to be anyone around to help me, so I walked over to it and signed my name. Next to my name they asked for my cell phone number. I was a little uncomfortable writing my number down there for everyone who came in after me to see, but the sign-up sheet stated that this information was required, so I did.

"I looked around for somewhere to sit and wait, but all of the plastic chairs that were jammed into a corner of the store were taken—and everyone there looked like they were about as tired as I was. I wondered about going next door to get a cup of coffee, but I was worried that they would call my name and I wouldn't be there, so I just leaned up against a wall. As I did so, I knocked a phone off its cradle, and it swung there beside me, tethered to the wall by a short cord. I picked it up and figured that I might as well make use of my time there by learning something about the phones. But when I looked at the plaque behind the phone cradle, there was just the name of the model—again all letters and numbers—and some technical specs for the phone—absolutely nothing about the phone itself or its user-friendly features. I punched a few buttons on the phone to see what I could learn that way, but it wasn't even powered up! I looked around the room, and there were tons of these phones tethered to the wall, all seemingly dead. I put the phone back on its cradle and slumped against the wall.

"As I stood there waiting (and waiting!) for my name to be called, I noticed that about every third name that was called, the person being called was no longer there—apparently they had gotten sick of waiting and just left. And every time it happened, the person who was calling the name didn't even note it anywhere—just crossed the name off as if the customer had been there and had been seen. I mean, isn't that something you should be tracking? That's a lot of people to just up and leave! Anyway, it seemed to be just an everyday occurrence that about a third of the people called were no longer there—none of the employees seemed to be surprised by this or pay any attention to it at all.

"Finally my name was called. I looked at my watch and it was 6:05—I had been waiting 35 minutes. But I figured that I could take care of this quickly and still make my dinner reservation. When I got up to the desk, I waited until the person behind the counter finished chatting about her weekend plans with someone else behind the counter. When she finally turned to me, I started explaining what I was there for. She looked confused, and then said, 'Oh, no—now I remember why I called you—it's not your turn yet, I just need to know why you wrote this cell number down on the sign-up sheet—it's not in our records.' When I explained that I wasn't a customer of theirs, so my number wouldn't be in their system, she asked why I had written my number on the sign-up sheet. I explained that the sign-up sheet indicated that this was required information, and that the number was, in fact, my cell phone number. When she stared at me blankly, I once again started to explain why I was there. She said, 'But I can't help you here if you're not a current customer. You'll have to go over there (she pointed across the room) and put your name on the SALES sign-up sheet.'

"I know you're going to think I'm crazy, but I actually did it—I walked across the room and signed-up at Sales, and went back and sat down—by this time there was a chair open. I can't explain why I stayed, other than to say that my daughter Rachel is a great kid, and she never asks for anything. I just really wanted to get her the phone she wanted. As I was sitting there waiting again, the woman next to me struck up a conversation. It turns out that she was there to cancel her service, and she had been waiting longer than I had. Apparently she had cancelled her service online more than three months ago, but a bill just kept coming in the mail. She finally decided that she had to come in and cancel it in person if it was ever going to actually get cancelled. The teenager on the other side of me said, 'Tell me about it. I bought a phone here a week ago, and they gave me the wrong phone charger with it. I'm just trying to get the right charger, and I've been here longer than either of you.' This prompted a comment from an aggravated customer three seats away, and another from a man leaning against the wall where I had been earlier. Once we had all vented our grievances, we settled in to wait. About 15 minutes later, a sales associate called my name.

"I walked up to the sales desk and had already started to explain what I was there for when I noticed that the sales associate was pointing to her ear and motioning that she was on the phone. I waited patiently while she made dinner plans with a friend, and I wondered how late I would be for my own dinner. When she finally turned to me, with a big smile on her face, I told her that I was looking for a phone that I had seen advertised a few days ago, and wondered if she could help me. She said, 'I have no idea what corporate is advertising these days—they never tell us that stuff.' So I told her that the model name was a bunch of letters and numbers, and that my daughter, who I was buying the phone for, said that it could do 'everything'—did she have any idea what model that would be? She said that she really had no idea, and maybe I should look around the store for a while and see if anything 'jumped out at me.'

"I told her that I had already looked at some phones and that none had 'jumped out at me,' and that maybe I should just buy one that I thought might be close, and then my daughter could bring it back and exchange it if it wasn't right. She said 'I don't think you can do that without paying a large fee, but maybe…I'm not really sure.' So I asked her if there was anyone in the store who MIGHT be sure. She said she would go check. When she came back out to the counter about five minutes later, she said that no one there was absolutely sure about the exchange policy on phones, and then she said with a big smile, 'OK, now I'm going to turn you over to Matthew—I know he'll take great care of you!' I asked her why she was 'turning me over to Matthew,' and she replied, 'It's seven o'clock, and that means I'm out of here! They pay us by the hour, so you better believe I'm not staying a minute past 7!' Again with the big, friendly smile. When I realized it was 7:00, I told Matthew, who was now standing in front of me, that I needed to call my wife and tell her I would be late for dinner. He said, 'That's cool, but then you better sign in again, because I need to take the next person on the list.' I put my phone back in my pocket and proceeded to retell everything I had already told the first sales associate to this new one, Matthew.

"When I had again finished my story, Matthew picked up a phone that was on the counter and said, 'Well, I like this phone—why don't you get her this one.' So I asked, 'Does it do *everything*?' and he replied, 'Sure.' So I gritted my teeth, slapped my credit card on the counter and said 'I'll take it.' Matthew gave me a six-page form and instructed me to go sit back over in the corner, fill out the form in its entirety, and bring it back when I had finished it, along with two forms of identification. I'm a little embarrassed to say that at that point I just wanted to get out of there, so I filled out the form (nowhere on this form was there any place to give customer feedback on the service that I had received), signed up for the shortest length of service possible, and took the phone as I ran out the door trying to call my wife and find my keys at the same time. As I was driving away, I realized that Matthew had not even suggested any of the peripherals my daughter would need—like a phone charger—but I decided that there was no way I was going back in there. I hoped I could pick up a phone charger somewhere else that would fit that phone.

"When I got home that evening, I went online to look at the CellularStar phones once again, still trying to figure out if the phone was the one Rachel wanted, and I saw that the online price for the model I had purchased was quite a bit lower than the price I had just paid at the store. So I called the store and asked to speak to Matthew, but the person on the phone told me that Matthew was busy packing up for the night, and that he couldn't help me. I told the person on the phone that I had found a lower price online than I had paid at the store that evening, and he just answered 'Oh, yeah.' When I asked him why, he said it was perfectly legal. Well, I wasn't asking whether it was legal! He then told me that if I had brought the online price to the salesperson's attention, the salesperson would have met the price—it was a new policy they had just instituted—but since I hadn't mentioned the online price during the sales transaction, I would have to pay the store price. So I said, 'Well, I'm mentioning it now!' and he said he was sorry, but as he understood it, they didn't have to give me the lower online price unless I mentioned the online price before buying the phone. So at this point, I just hung up.

"The next day at work, I was telling someone about this awful experience with CellularStar, and they said that they thought we had a corporate rep from CellularStar assigned to our company—apparently you guys have been trying to get our company business for a few years now. So I called around and got his name, and gave him a call. He didn't call me back for hours, but he did call at the end of the day—I was pleased that he got back to me the same business day. I told him about my experience with CellularStar, and when I finished, he said that since he was not involved in that part of the business, there wasn't anything he could do—he only dealt with corporate accounts. When I asked who I should be calling to complain, he said he didn't know—again explaining that he really didn't have anything to do with 'that end of the business.' But interestingly, the next day I received an e-mail from the CellularStar corporate rep with an attachment that was a long and indecipherable list of corporate rates and schedules—none of which I qualified for, since my company wasn't a current customer of his!

"When the first bill came, I noticed that the monthly charge was not what I thought I had signed up for—it was quite a bit higher, and seemed to include a fee for something I had never seen before. The description line for this additional fee was an acronym that made no sense to me. I spent 10 minutes reading all the pages of fine print and still could not figure out what that acronym meant. I got back on the CellularStar website, hoping to find a page that would decode the bill in English. No such luck. So again I called the service line, and made my way through the IVR and the 20 minutes of hold time. When I finally spoke to a customer service rep, he could not even tell me what that acronym stood for!

"It was then that I decided to try to cancel my contract with CellularStar, return the phone, and try to recoup any money I could from this horrible experience. I dreaded the return trip to the CellularStar store, and I was really angry that after all my effort, I still was not going to be able to give my daughter what she wanted for her 13th birthday. I hadn't felt this much anger in a long time. I had been telling everyone I knew about the really awful way that CellularStar treats its customers, and I was about to go to Epinions.com and tell the world about my horrible experience with CellularStar. I just really wanted to vent about everything. And let's face it, every step of the way I had tried to tell people at CellularStar what was going on, but no one was *listening*!

"I don't mean to tell you how to run your business, but I know that at my business, we live and die by customer feedback. We collect feedback from them every step of the way, everything from the big, overarching customer feedback mechanisms—Net Promoter Scores and customer satisfaction surveys—to just about anything else that allows us to gauge how things are going for the customer. The front-line people are constantly gathering feedback from customers, and the marketing people are putting this feedback in some format that means something to the rest of us in the company— we *always* know how we're doing in the eyes of the customer. And my job is nowhere near the front line, but you better believe that my bonus is tied to how happy our customers are.

"Anyway, as I was composing something to post online, I realized there might be one other means of contacting your company that I hadn't thought of—the good old-fashioned complaint letter. So I went back to the CellularStar web page and looked for the CEO's address. When it wasn't there, I called the service line, waited through the IVR and 20 minutes of hold time *again*, and finally got someone who reluctantly gave me your CEO's name and the address at headquarters. And, well, here I am.

"The funny thing is, my wife works for another business in our city—the largest company in the city in fact—and she works in purchasing. A couple of weeks after my initial contact with CellularStar, the same corporate account rep that I had been trying like crazy to get some information out of, called on my wife at work. Her company's contract with one of your competitors was about to end, and he wanted to see if she would be willing to sign her company on with CellularStar. My wife told me that she let him go on for quite some time about CellularStar's commitment to 'Convenience' and 'Service'—he even had a lapel pin with your tagline, 'Cellular Convenience, Star Service'! Finally she told him my story. He didn't even remember me! And she said that when she reiterated every detail of my story, he just sat there—he made no attempt to write anything down or look into why these things had happened. At the end of the meeting, he said he hoped that she would join the CellularStar 'family,' shook her hand, and left. I swear to you, I'm not making this stuff up.

"Oh, and three weeks—three weeks—after I sent that initial e-mail question out to CellularStar, I received a curt answer from someone saying that they couldn't share any information regarding their advertising schedules with me. And at the bottom of the e-mail, there was that tagline again—'Cellular Convenience, Star Service.'"

After the morning interview with Hal, the team thanked him profusely and sent him back to his hotel, asking him to please come back the following morning to meet with the team once again before he flew home. The team then went out to lunch together, but everyone had a hard time eating; it was hard to process all of the information they had received from Hal, and hard to accept how really awful his experience with CellularStar had been. Most of the executives on the team had, up until that morning, believed that they provided their customers with a fairly positive experience.

After a lot of silence, one of your team members, Ted, finally said, "I think we should approach this information from a Customer Experience Management standpoint. We've all been learning a great deal about the process of CEM. Let's see if we can't try to apply the process to the customer experience we've just heard about. We can use this as a sort of trial run for the full-blown CEM project that we are about to undertake. I know that it will only be based on one customer's experience with our brand, but I think the exercise of trying to apply CEM concepts to this one customer's experience will teach us a lot. Anyway, it's better than sitting around moping about what we've just heard! I think we should apply the tenets of CEM to what we know about Hal's experience, and I think we should complete this mini-project today. That way, we can present our results to Hal in the morning and get his feedback."

Most of the team members agreed to cancel their afternoon meetings and work on this project. They decided to reconvene in an hour to begin work. Because Ted had, since the formation of the cross-functional team, been the most interested in CEM and had done quite a bit of individual background research, he agreed to be the one to articulate the challenges as he understood them, and facilitate the team as it approached this abbreviated project.

When the group reconvened an hour later, Ted presented the following challenges:

1. Map the customer journey with regard to CellularStar, including all customer-brand interactions, or "Touch Points."

The first phase of a customer experience mapping process is focused on attaining a comprehensive understanding of every touch point between the brand and the customer (e.g., marketing communications and promotions, word of mouth, direct channels such as website and call center interactions, point-of-sale interactions, service provision, postpurchase interactions, etc.). We should make sure that this map reflects the realities of our particular customers and, in this case, specifically Hal's experience.   It must also be comprehensive. In the reading I've done on Customer Experience Management, I have seen examples of 10-foot-long maps posted outside of executives' offices. Obviously, since our map will be based on just one customer's experience, ours will not be extremely lengthy, but I think it will be good practice for us to attempt to capture our one customer's experience as comprehensively as possible.

2. Map that same customer journey as it would look if all interactions were optimal, and compare this new optimal experience map with the customer experience map developed in step 1.

This requires us to create a vision of what the optimal customer experience would look like. We should start by taking each touch point of the customer experience map that we've created in step 1 and, for each of these, envisioning the best possible interaction from the customer's point of view. We'll have to use our judgment on this, since Hal is not here to consult with us this afternoon. Tomorrow morning, we'll show him the results of this process—the customer experience map, the optimal experience map, and our ideas regarding changes that could be made to enhance the customer experience—and ask for his feedback.

3. Identify changes that would enhance the customer experience with CellularStar, and prioritize those changes.

After comparing the customer experience map with the optimal experience map, we should brainstorm ways in which we can close the gap between the two. This requires us to brainstorm changes that we could make that would potentially eliminate or soften dissatisfiers in the customer experience (Hal's long wait time at our retail store would be an obvious example of a dissatisfier). We should also look for those parts of the customer journey where we have an opportunity to go above and beyond what the customer expects, thereby delighting the customer and enhancing his overall experience with CellularStar.

Once we have brainstormed all possible changes, we must choose those that have the most potential to positively impact the overall customer experience, and that are feasible to implement. Again, because the customer—Hal—is not present, we'll have to use our judgment on this and ask for feedback from him tomorrow. We should list each potential change and describe the specific redesigns within the company that these changes would likely encompass. We may find that there are some "quick fixes" that we would be comfortable making based on the information we have to date. After we have identified "quick fixes" and decided whether or not to implement them, we then need to prioritize the more complex changes that we have identified. Like most companies, we don't have unlimited resources, and we must therefore decide where to invest our limited resources in redesigning the customer experience.

4. Align company processes, policies, support systems, and employees with the changes that have been chosen for implementation.

Let's assume that we choose to implement the top three significant (not "quick fix") changes that we have prioritized in step 3 of this process. Then we must describe (or reiterate, if we have already done so) the necessary redesigns regarding company employees, processes, policies, and support systems that this change would likely encompass. Given the criticality of employee "buy-in" to Customer Experience Management, we should pay particular attention to the suggestions that we make regarding properly educating employees, empowering them, and changing incentive programs and performance measures to reflect a focus on the customer experience.

Please do the following:

Address each of the four challenges delineated by Ted. Please note that whereas true Customer Experience Management efforts are highly dependent upon continuing input from the customer, this hypothetical situation does not allow for the very important element of ongoing customer communication. For this reason, you must use a good deal of "executive judgment" in your answers. Please make every attempt to use realistic suppositions based on the one description of Hal's customer experience and what you have learned regarding the customer experience mapping process. The value of this case rests in its potential to introduce you to the underutilized and very powerful process of customer experience mapping. Note that this process is not always hierarchical and may involve some "looping back" from a later phase of the process to an earlier one as you complete this abbreviated customer experience mapping project.

References:

Bottomley, M. (2003, December 8). *Brand Transformation Through Customer Experience Management.* Retrieved December 10, 2008, from CRM Project: www.crmproject.com.

Meyer, C., & Schwager, A. (2007). "Understanding Customer Experience." *Harvard Business Review.*

Rickard, D. (2006). *Winning by Understanding the Full Customer Experience: Opportunities for Action in Industrial Goods.* The Boston Consulting Group.

Strativity Group, Inc. (2008). *Customer Experience Management Benchmark Study.* Rochelle Park, NJ: Strativity Group, Inc.

SECTION II:

CUSTOMER PERCEPTION

4. Information Overload

Information Overload occurs when too much information is presented to a consumer and the consumer has difficulty processing it all. The "working memory," or that part of the mind that processes incoming information, is subject to very real capacity limitations. The working memory can typically handle up to about seven items of information at one time (under the best of circumstances). If the amount of information exceeds that capacity, *Information Overload* occurs, and the processing capability is denigrated—sometimes severely reducing the amount of incoming information that can be processed.

Please follow the instructions for this exercise carefully, and in the order in which they are given.

Step One: Within your team of two, decide which team member will be the Reader and which team member will be the Responder.

Step Two: If you are the Responder, close your book and wait for instructions from the Reader. If you are the Reader, continue to follow these directions.

Step Three (Reader only): Fill in the following seven blanks with any seven digits, in any order (try to avoid obvious patterns—the more random the order, the better). Do not let the Responder see what you are writing.

___-___-___-___-___-___-___

Step Four (Reader only): Read the following instructions to the Responder:
> "*I am about to read to you a series of numbers. When I finish, please repeat the series to the best of your ability.*"

Don't allow the Responder to see the numbers, and don't allow him/her to write the numbers down. Read the digits to the Responder, then look up and wait for the Responder's response.

Step Five (Reader only): Note how successful the Responder was in remembering and successfully repeating the numbers in the order given. If he/she was not able to repeat them all successfully, which ones were remembered? Which ones were lost? Circle the numbers that the Responder was able to successfully remember and repeat in the order given.

Step Six (Reader only): Repeat *Steps Three, Four, and Five*, but this time use a series of 11 digits:

___-___-___-___-___-___-___-___-___-___-___

Remember to note how successful the Responder was in remembering and successfully repeating the numbers in the order given.

Step Seven (Both Reader and Responder): Reader and Responder should discuss with one another the results of this exercise.

Discussion Questions:
Compare the results of the 7-digit test with the results of the 11-digit test. If the Responder was not able to repeat all the digits in the 11-digit test, which ones were lost? Did he/she remember as many digits in the 11-digit test as he/she did in the 7-digit test (for example, if in the first test the Responder was able to successfully repeat all 7 digits in the order given, was he/she then able to successfully repeat AT LEAST the first 7 of the 11-digit test)?

Step Eight (Optional): Repeat the previous steps, but change roles. The Reader will now act as the Responder, and the Responder will now take on the role of the Reader, so that each student has the opportunity to experience *Information Overload.*

5. The Just Noticeable Difference

The Just Noticeable Difference (aka the "jnd") is the minimum amount of change in a stimulus that can be detected. Using sound as an example, if a decibel level change from 60 decibels to 62 decibels is undetectable and a change from 60 decibels to 63 decibels can be detected, we know that at an initial stimulus of 60 decibels, a change of 3 decibels is the Just Noticeable Difference.

Over 100 years ago, a psychophysicist named Ernst Weber found that the amount of change necessary to be discernable is not an absolute amount, but is related to the initial intensity of the stimulus. For example, discounting a $50.00 shirt by $5.00 may not be perceived by consumers as a meaningful change in price, but discounting a $25.00 shirt by $5.00 likely would. Therefore, the Just Noticeable Difference is often described as a percentage. Apparel retailers have found that discounting the price of a garment by less than 20% does not usually result in consumers' perception of a meaningful change in price, but discounting the garment by 20% usually does result in the perception of a meaningful change in price.

Some marketers have recently suggested renaming this phenomenon as the "Just Meaningful Difference (jmd)" to highlight the fact that the Just Noticeable Difference should not only be discernable to the consumer, but should also signify a *meaningful* change. In the example above, consumers would surely be able to perceive that the price of a $50.00 shirt discounted by $5.00 has changed, but they would likely not perceive the discount as meaningful. This argument for renaming the "Just Noticeable Difference" as the "Just Meaningful Difference" brings up an important point: In order for a change to affect consumer behavior, it must be noticed *and* perceived as meaningful. For the purposes of this case, we will use the traditional term Just Noticeable Difference, but it should be noted that in a marketing context, the Just Noticeable Difference must be both noticed and perceived as meaningful by the consumer.

Another important point about the Just Noticeable Difference involves the application of the concept. Strictly speaking, the concept of the Just Noticeable Difference implies that one need not go beyond the Just Noticeable Difference in order to affect consumer behavior. In other words, if the Just Noticeable Difference is 5%, one must only change a stimulus by 5% in order to affect consumer behavior; changing the stimulus by more than that amount is typically not cost effective. As an example, in the case of decreasing the price of a product, if a marketer significantly exceeds the decrease dictated by the Just Noticeable Difference, he/she is "giving away" more than is necessary. Simply meeting the Just Noticeable Difference would have been enough to alert consumers that a meaningful change in the price has taken place, and, according to this theory, affect their behavior.

Part 1

Harry and Garry are twin brothers, and they each own appliance stores. Harry lives in Raleigh, North Carolina, and Garry lives in Tampa, Florida. Even though they live far apart, they talk often, and trade hints and grievances about the appliance retail business. Lately, they have been discussing the fact that in a tough economy consumers often hold off on the upgrade of an appliance as long as possible, deciding that they will wait to "trade up" when the economy turns around or the appliance breaks, whichever comes first. The brothers are discussing the wisdom of instituting short-term rebates in order to make their appliances more attractive to consumers, and to increase their rather dismal recent sales figures.

Unbeknownst to each other, both Harry and Garry decide to institute a retail-level rebate on a specific high-end stove. The price of the stove in both stores is $1,000, and both Harry and Garry's rebate offers will be advertised in the Sunday paper, and will last one week. Neither Harry nor Garry has done the research necessary to discover the Just Noticeable Difference (which, for that target market and that product category in that economic climate, is 15%). Harry offers consumers a $100 rebate on the $1,000 stove. Garry offers consumers a $200 rebate on the $1,000 stove. Harry sells 20 stoves during the rebate period, which is about the same number that he sold the week just prior to the rebate offer. Garry sells 30 stoves during the rebate period, which is an increase of about 10 more than he sold the week just prior to the rebate offer.

Did *the fact that he didn't know the accurate Just Noticeable Difference* cost Harry any money? Yes/No (circle one).   If yes, how much? _____.

Did *the fact that he didn't know the accurate Just Noticeable Difference* cost Garry any money? Yes/No (circle one).   If yes, how much? _____.

Part 2 (New Scenario)

You work for a large health food marketer, and you are responsible for the cereal line. One of your products is a raisin bran that comes in a 20-ounce box and currently sells at the retail level for $5.00. The raw materials costs for this product have increased significantly recently, all but eating up your profit margin. Your chief marketing officer (CMO) is now telling you that the retail price of the cereal has to be increased from 25 cents an ounce to 30 cents an ounce within the next year, or she will seriously consider deleting that product from the company's product mix.

Given the level of price competition in this product category, you know that consumers will definitely notice and perceive as meaningful an increase in the price of your cereal from $5.00 to $6.00. In fact, your research tells you that your target consumers' Just Noticeable Difference for food products in this category is 12%.

You know you need to do what your CMO has demanded, so you make the price change that will result in an increase in the retail price of the 20-ounce box of cereal from $5.00 to $6.00, and you schedule the price change to take effect within the month. What other alternative(s) do you have?

(Hint: there are at least two distinct and different alternatives available to you).

6. Perceptual Maps

The construction of a perceptual map helps marketing strategists better understand the positioning of their product/service, and the positioning of their competitors' products/services. A product's position, of course, is the way in which consumers perceive a product on important features relative to competing products.

As a very simplified example, if a marketer is interested in how her brand of beer (brand A) and two competing brands of beer (brands B and C) are perceived by target consumers, she might ask consumers to answer questions such as:

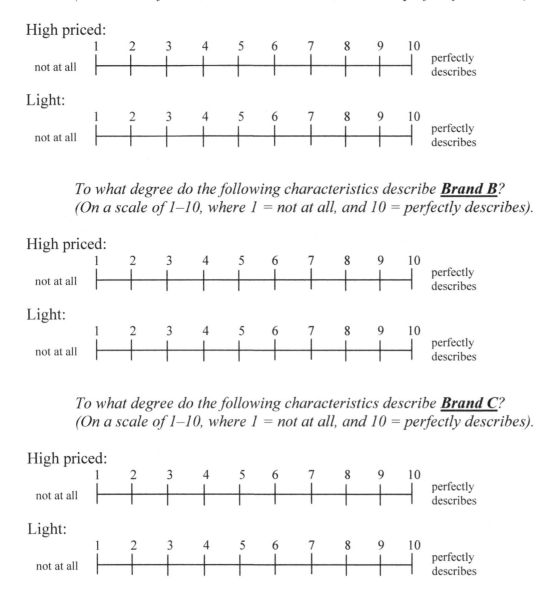

*To what degree do the following characteristics describe **Brand A**?*
(On a scale of 1–10, where 1 = not at all, and 10 = perfectly describes).

High priced:

Light:

*To what degree do the following characteristics describe **Brand B**?*
(On a scale of 1–10, where 1 = not at all, and 10 = perfectly describes).

High priced:

Light:

*To what degree do the following characteristics describe **Brand C**?*
(On a scale of 1–10, where 1 = not at all, and 10 = perfectly describes).

High priced:

Light:

If the target market being investigated is fairly homogenous, and so averaging the responses would not forego important data, she can look at the average responses by consumers in this target segment, and plot those mean responses on a two-dimensional map. For instance, if Brand A received an average response of 8 on the "high priced" dimension and 3 on the "light" dimension, and Brand B received an average response of 3 on the "high priced" dimension and 2 on the "light" dimension, and Brand C received an average response of 5 on the "high priced" dimension and 4 on the "light" dimension, she could plot these mean responses as follows:

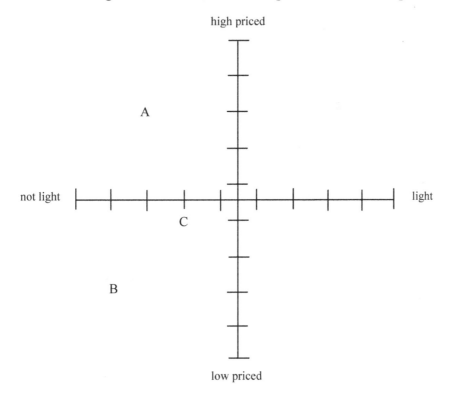

Although the above is obviously a very simplified example, perceptual maps can be quite useful when investigating consumer perceptions of many different brands on many different attributes. In general, software systems are used to plot these results in multidimensional space. The number of dimensions of a perceptual map is equal to the number of attributes that are investigated in a perceptual mapping application.

In the simplified example above, there are just two product attributes: high priced and light. So in this example, the resulting data can easily be plotted in two-dimensional space. However, most perceptual mapping applications involve more than two product attributes, and when this is the case, creative plotting strategies are needed to represent the multidimensional data results in two-dimensional space. Many times, vectors or lines are used to represent the many different attributes, and the distance between each brand and the attribute line denotes the degree to which consumers perceive that attribute as describing that brand. For example, consider the amount of information that appears in the perceptual map recreated on the next page.[1] In this example, the authors have attempted to visually represent a large number of armchair types (in this case, the armchairs can be thought of as the different brands) on a large number of attributes.

_____

[1] Chuang, Y., & Chen, L.-L. (2008). "How to Rate 100 Visual Stimuli," *International Journal of Design.*

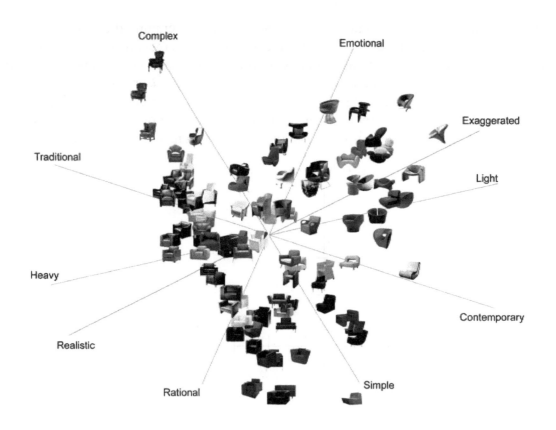

Complex
Emotional
Exaggerated
Light
Traditional
Contemporary
Heavy
Realistic
Rational
Simple

Source: Chuang, Y., & Chen, L.-L. (2008). "How to Rate 100 Visual Stimuli," *International Journal of Design.*

Many of the current perceptual mapping software systems utilize a type of factor analysis in their analysis of data such that when the different brands are all perceived in the same way on an attribute, that attribute is deleted, since it generates no new information. In other words, because all brands are perceived in exactly the same way on that attribute, the inclusion of the attribute does not contribute any information to an understanding of the relative positioning of brands, and so the attribute falls out of the data mix.

This approach also results in the combination of two or more attributes if the data related to those attributes are highly correlated. If, for example, when consumers are responding to questions regarding attributes of winter tires, they perceive the attribute "handling" in exactly the same way as the attribute "traction" across all rated brands, it is likely that these two attributes are viewed by the consumer as one and the same. In this case, the two highly correlated attributes should be combined into one attribute, since the data from one attribute merely mimics the other, providing no new information. Often when this is done, the resulting combined attribute is given an appropriate name, such as "handling and traction."

Part 1

You are responsible for a brand of frozen pizza. You have four close competitors in the region, and you are interested in obtaining a better understanding of consumers' perceptions of all five frozen pizzas (Brands A, B, C, D, E) on four product attributes: nutritional content, price, freshness of ingredients, and doughy crust. You survey a large number of members of your target market segment, young moms, with the following question format:

> *To what degree do the following characteristics describe (**insert—Brand A, B, C, D, E**)?*
> *(On a scale of 1—10, where 1 = not at all, and 10 = perfectly describes).*
> *(**Attribute—insert one: high nutritional content, high price, fresh ingredients, doughy crust**):*
>
> ```
>            1    2    3    4    5    6    7    8    9   10
> not at all |----|----|----|----|----|----|----|----|----|    perfectly
>                                                               describes
> ```

*(**Such that all five brands are rated on all four attributes.**)*

The resulting data are fairly consistent among respondents, meaning that this particular target market segment is fairly homogeneous in its perceptions of frozen pizzas. Therefore, you feel comfortable averaging responses. The results of the survey, with average responses rounded to the nearest whole number, are displayed below:

Attributes	Brand A	Brand B	Brand C	Brand D	Brand E
Nutrition	9	2	7	4	3
Price	5	5	5	5	5
Ingredients	9	2	7	4	3
Crust	3	7	1	9	2

Please create a perceptual map for these results in the space below.

Part 2

Your boss has asked you to brainstorm growth strategies for the coming year, and has specifically asked that you evaluate the profitability of extending the frozen pizza line to include more varieties. He is wondering if there may be opportunities in the marketplace that have not yet been addressed by any currently existing product offering. He would prefer not to cannibalize your existing company brand (Brand A), and if possible, would prefer not to compete "head-to-head" with any competing brand (Brands B, C, D, or E), since the struggle to win market share by competing directly with an existing competing product is typically a very costly undertaking.

Do you see any potential growth opportunities in the perceptual map you created in Part 1 that would meet your boss' criteria? Please describe the opportunity(ies).

Do you have enough information now to make the decision to pursue this opportunity? What other information do you need in order to assess whether this potential opportunity might be worth pursuing?

Part 3

Once a potential growth opportunity has been identified on a perceptual map, more information must be collected. It is possible that there are no existing products in a particular area of a perceptual map for good reason. It may be that there are no products in that product space because there is not a viable market for that type of product. For example, in looking at the armchair example, one sees a potential opportunity in the space that could be described as an extremely "Realistic" design. However, whereas that type of armchair could certainly be marketed, the demand for the chair may be so low that there is no real opportunity there. In other words, it is possible that there is no existing armchair design in that area of the map simply because there is not sufficient demand for that type of armchair; no one *wants* an armchair that is extremely "Realistic" in design.

When assessing an opportunity on a perceptual map, one must evaluate whether sufficient consumer demand exists for a product that would fill the product space indicated by the potential opportunity.

In the beer example used at the start of this case, let's imagine that the marketer asks *one specific consumer* the following questions:

> *With regard to beer, my <u>ideal product</u> would be:*
> *(On a scale of 1–10, where 1 = not at all, and 10 = perfectly describes).*

High priced:

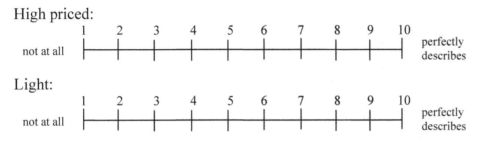

(Please note that whereas it is tempting to make assumptions about ideal points, this can often get a marketer into trouble. For example, in the above, it may seem obvious that a consumer would want a beer that is "not at all" high priced. However, in reality there are many consumers who prefer to drink a high priced beer for the status that it confers.)

If, in this overly simplified beer example, this *one specific consumer* answered 2 to the "high priced" question and 9 to the "light" question, that specific consumer's "Ideal Point" (symbolized by *I*) could be plotted on the map as follows:

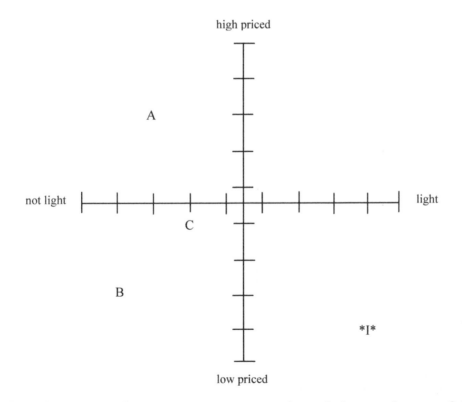

It appears that this *one specific consumer's* ideal (*I*) is not being met by any of the existing brands of beer (brands A, B, or C). This may indicate a market opportunity if, and only if, a sufficient number of consumers share that one specific consumer's "Ideal Point," thus making the demand for a new beer (that addresses this ideal point) large enough to be profitable. In other words, if this one specific consumer's ideal with regard to beer is only shared by a few other target consumers, the opportunity may not be viable, since the demand would not be great enough to warrant the development of a new product. On the other hand, if there are a large number of target consumers who share that vision of the ideal beer, it may be profitable to develop a new product that meets their needs.

By surveying a large number of target consumers about their ideals with regard to a product category, one can begin to see the different clusters of consumer demand that exist. This is, in effect, a way of segmenting consumers by benefits sought. Typically, there are segments of consumers with similar ideal points forming clusters. These clusters, or consumer segments, are plotted in different parts of the map to indicate the location of each segment's ideal point. In some product categories, all consumer ideal points are very similar, resulting in one large cluster at a specific point on the map. But for most product categories, different segments of consumers possess quite different ideal points—if this were not the case, we would all drive the same car!

The size of each cluster depicted on the map is used to indicate the relative size of that consumer segment. A map that represents many ideal point clusters, or consumer segments, is called a preference map. A hypothetical preference map for the beer example is shown below:

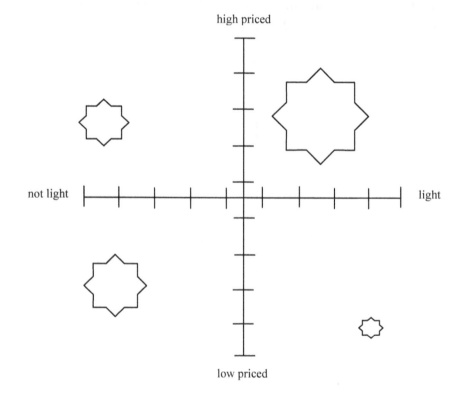

If we compare the perceptual map and the preference map for the beer example, we can see how consumer perceptions of existing beer brands on these two attributes match up with various consumer segments' ideal points with regard to those attributes. We also have a visual representation of the relative size of each cluster/consumer segment.

Given this very simplified beer example, please answer the following questions:

1. As brand manager for Brand A beer, which competitor, Brand B or Brand C, is your closest competitor?

2. As brand manager for Brand A beer, what opportunities and threats do you see highlighted by the perceptual and preference maps?

3. What else have you learned from the two maps?

SECTION III:

CUSTOMER LEARNING AND MEMORY

7. Behavioral Learning: Classical and Operant Conditioning

Classical Conditioning and Operant (Instrumental) Conditioning are well-known behavioral theories of learning, and both are central to an understanding of consumer behavior. This critical thinking exercise is designed to aid in the understanding of the two behavioral theories, and enhance students' ability to recognize the types of marketing situations in which one or the other form of conditioning might occur.

Operant (Instrumental) Conditioning

The basic premise of Operant Conditioning is very straightforward: Those behaviors that are rewarded are more likely to be repeated, and those behaviors that are punished are less likely to be repeated. An overt action (*Behavior* in the figure below) leads to some reinforcement or punishment (*Consequence* in the figure below), which then leads to an increase (if reinforced) or decrease (if punished) in the probability that the behavior will be repeated.

Behavior ⟶ Consequence ⟶ Increased or Decreased Probability of Behavior

In many marketing situations, the behavior is an action such as the purchase of a product or shopping at a particular store, and the consequence is a reward in the form of some sales promotion (e.g., a premium or discount) which then increases the likelihood that the consumer will repeat the original behavior. A positive experience with a product (e.g., satisfaction) can also be seen as a reinforcer.

Classical Conditioning

This theory of Classical Conditioning proposes that a neutral object (something with little inherent meaning to a consumer, e.g., a low-involvement product) can be associated with a meaningful object or concept, and through this association consumers can learn to respond to the neutral object in the same way that they respond to the meaningful object.

In a marketing context, the meaningful "*Unconditioned Stimulus*" is typically something that will cause a predictable and positive response in consumers (the "*Unconditioned Response*" in the figure on the next page). For example, the *Unconditioned Stimulus* might be the use of humor in an ad, which results in an *Unconditioned Response* of good feelings. By associating this meaningful *Unconditioned Stimulus* (e.g., humor) with a *Neutral Stimulus* (e.g., a product) through repeated pairings (usually via advertising), the consumer "learns" to respond to the *Neutral Stimulus* in the same way that they responded to the *Unconditioned Stimulus*, even in the absence of the *Unconditioned Stimulus*. Once this association has been successfully learned, the *Neutral Stimulus* is then called the *Conditioned Stimulus*, and the *Unconditioned Response* is called the *Conditioned Response* (see figure on the next page).

Unconditioned
Stimulus

Neutral
Stimulus

After Repeated Pairings:

Unconditioned
Response

(becomes)

(becomes)

Conditioned
Stimulus

Conditioned
Response

In essence, there are three separate and distinct components to this theory, since the *Neutral Stimulus* becomes the *Conditioned Stimulus*, and the *Unconditioned Response* becomes the *Conditioned Response*. We will call these three separate components the *Unconditioned Stimulus*, the *Neutral/Conditioned Stimulus*, and the *Unconditioned/Conditioned Response*.

Please do the following:

Below you will find two examples and then six scenarios involving conditioning principles in a marketing context. Once you have read and understood the two examples, turn your attention to each of the scenarios. For each of the scenarios given, state whether Operant (Instrumental) Conditioning principles or Classical Conditioning principles are involved by <u>underlining</u> the appropriate theory. Then identify the components of the theory using the blank spaces provided under that theory. The first two examples have been completed for you (with descriptions of the reasoning process behind the answers) in order to clarify the suggested process.

EXAMPLES

Example 1. While he is shopping at his local discount store, Jack's attention is called to a product on "in-store special." He buys the product on special, and is pleased to receive a $10.00 savings on his purchase. The next time he is shopping in that environment, he is more likely to purchase the in-store specials.

<u>**Operant Conditioning**</u>

Behavior:__purchase "special" prod.

Consequence:___$10.00 savings___

Expected Change:__increased___
    purchasing of products on special

Classical Conditioning

Uncond.Stimulus:_____

Neutral/Cond. Stimulus:_____

Uncond./Cond. Response:_____

Reasoning: This situation can be understood from an Operant Conditioning perspective in the following way: The consumer behavior of purchasing a product on special led to the positive, reinforcing consequence of savings. This positive consequence is expected to increase the likelihood that the consumer will purchase products on special in the future.

Example 2. **Every time Sue sees that hilarious commercial for Champion's Pizza, it makes her laugh and feel good. When she sees a sign for Champion's Pizza while driving, she smiles.**

Operant Conditioning	**Classical Conditioning**
Behavior:_____	Uncond. Stimulus:_____humor_____
Consequence:_____	Neutral/Cond. Stimulus: _Champion's Pizza_
Expected Change:_____	Uncond./Cond. Response:__good feelings_

Reasoning: This situation can be understood from a Classical Conditioning perspective in the following way: The Unconditioned Stimulus of humor is expected to result in the Unconditioned Response of good feelings. When the humor is paired repeatedly (through advertising) with the Neutral Stimulus, Champion's Pizza, an association is formed between the humor and Champion's Pizza. Through this association, the consumer "learns" to respond to Champion's Pizza in the same way that she responded to the humor, and this response no longer depends upon the presence of the humor.

Please note that the Unconditioned/Conditioned Response in Classical Conditioning is rarely more specific than "good feelings" or "positive emotions."

When completing the six scenarios that follow, students need only underline the appropriate theory and fill in the related components; *no description of reasoning is required.* Of the six scenarios to be completed, three illustrate Classical Conditioning, and three illustrate Operant (Instrumental) Conditioning.

SCENARIOS

1. Bob likes to stop and get coffee every morning on his way to work. He has a frequency customer card, so every 10th coffee order is free. He is much too busy to keep track of how many "points" he has to date, but he is pleasantly surprised when he is told that his morning coffee will be free of charge. In the future, he vows to stop at that coffee shop rather than the other one he sometimes frequents.

Operant Conditioning	Classical Conditioning
Behavior: PURCHASE COFFEE	Uncond. Stimulus:_____
Consequence: ONE/TEN FREE	Neutral/Cond. Stimulus:_____
Expected Change: INCREASE	Uncond./Cond. Response:_____
PURCHASE IN THAT	
LOCATION.	

2. Whenever Richard hears the nostalgic music that plays in the background of the Charge Cola ad, it makes him remember his buddies from high school and some of the good times he had with them. When he goes to the grocery store to do the shopping for his family, he scans the soda aisle, then chooses Charge Cola rather than all the other similar sodas; he just feels best about the Charge Cola brand.

Operant Conditioning

Behavior:_____

Consequence:_____

Expected Change:_____

Classical Conditioning

Uncond. Stimulus: _MUSIC_

Neutral/Cond. Stimulus: _CHARGE COLA_

Uncond./Cond. Response: _GOOD FEELING ABOUT THE COLA BRAND_

---

3. Shelly loves the commercial for Cloud tissues, because she really likes seeing the fuzzy little puppies in the ad romping around. At the drug store, she never considers another brand of tissue—she just assumes that Cloud is the softest brand.

Operant Conditioning

Behavior:_____

Consequence:_____

Expected Change:_____

Classical Conditioning

Uncond. Stimulus: _FUZZY PUPPIES_

Neutral/Cond. Stimulus: _CLOUD TISSUE_

Uncond./Cond. Response: _PURCHASE BRAND_

---

4. When wandering through the frozen food section of her grocery store, Mary noticed a new frozen pizza. She bought the frozen pizza and tried it for dinner that night. Mary was very pleased with the pizza, and thought it was the best pizza she had ever tasted. She put it on her shopping list to buy again.

Operant Conditioning

Behavior: _GROCERY SHOPPING_

Consequence: _TASTE BEST PIZZA_

Expected Change: _REPEAT PURCHASE_

Classical Conditioning

Uncond. Stimulus:_____

Neutral/Cond. Stimulus:_____

Uncond./Cond. Response:_____

---

5. Whenever Ralph saw the print advertisements for Smith's Spark Plugs he couldn't help but notice how attractive the bikini-clad models in the ad were. When he needed new spark plugs for his car, he didn't put much thought into which brand he would buy—he just liked the Smith brand.

Operant Conditioning

Behavior:_____

Consequence:_____

Expected Change:_____

Classical Conditioning

Uncond. Stimulus: _BIKINI-CLAD MODEL_

Neutral/Cond. Stimulus: _SPARK PLUG_

Uncond./Cond. Response: _GOOD FEELINGS TOWARD THE SMITH BRAND_

---

6. Julie was shopping at the mall when the grand opening celebration of a new bookstore caught her eye. She wandered in and one of the store clerks handed her a complementary gift—a lovely journal. Although she didn't need to purchase any books that day, she will stop back in to that store the next time she is in the mall.

Operant Conditioning	Classical Conditioning
Behavior: _WANDERING IN MALL_	Uncond. Stimulus: _____
Consequence: _GIFT IN BOOKSTORE_	Neutral/Cond. Stimulus: _____
Expected Change: _RETURN TO STORE_	Uncond./Cond. Response: _____

----

8. Memorable Taglines

In the UK, they are called endlines. In Belgium, they are called baselines. In Italy, they are called payoffs. In France, they are called signatures. In the United States, they are called taglines. To further complicate matters, some draw a distinction between slogans and taglines (aka endlines/payoffs, etc.), and some use the words interchangeably. We'll simplify matters and call them all taglines. At their best, taglines can be a powerful asset to your brand, and at their worst, they can be a waste of time and money. Taglines work by triggering important brand associations in consumers' minds and making your brand more memorable. What makes a tagline effective and memorable?

Task 1—Matching the Tagline to the Brand

Please match the tagline on the left with a company/product/brand on the right, by placing the name of the company/product/brand from the right in the blank that appears by or in the tagline. Each tagline should be matched with one and only one company/product/brand. It should be noted that many of the taglines you see here are U.S.-based (reflecting the experience of the author); my apologies to those of you who are not as familiar with these particular taglines.

(Once you have completed the task, refer the answer key at the end of this case to see how you did.)

There's always room for _____.	Burger King
The ultimate driving machine._____	Timex
Generation next._____	GEICO Insurance
Wait till we get our _____ on you.	MasterCard
Got _____?	Bounty
Takes a licking and keeps on ticking._____	Nike
Just do it._____	Vegas (Las Vegas)
Like a rock._____	Pringles potato chips
Have it your way._____	Hanes
Because I'm worth it._____	JELL-O
Don't leave home without it._____	Pepsi
You're in good hands._____	Chevrolet
Keeps on going and going…_____	M&Ms
Nothing runs like a _____.	L'Oréal
_____: the quicker picker-upper.	Subway restaurants
Melts in your mouth, not in your hands.____	Energizer batteries
Priceless._____	Allstate Insurance
Expect more. Pay less._____	BMW
Eat fresh._____	Target
15 minutes could save you 15%._____	Milk
Once you pop, you can't stop._____	American Express
What happens in _____ stays in _____.	Deere (John Deere tractors)

44

How did you do when identifying the tagline "The Ultimate Driving Machine"? How about "Generation next"? Would you have identified "The Ultimate Driving Machine" even if it was a stand-alone question (not a matching exercise with answers provided)? Did you correctly identify "Generation next" only through the process of elimination?

Al Ries, writing for *Advertising Age*,[1] notes that in the 33 years "since 1975, BMW has used one tagline: 'The Ultimate Driving Machine.' On the other hand, since 1975 Pepsi-Cola has used these advertising taglines:
> 1975: 'For those who think young.'
> 1978: 'Have a Pepsi day.'
> 1980: 'Catch the Pepsi spirit.'
> 1982: 'Pepsi's got your taste for life.'
> 1983: 'Pepsi now.'
> 1984: 'The choice of a new generation.'
> 1989: 'A generation ahead.'
> 1990: 'Pepsi: The choice of a new generation.'
> 1992: 'Gotta have it.'
> 1993: 'Be young. Have fun. Drink Pepsi.'
> 1995: 'Nothing else is a Pepsi.'
> 2002: 'Generation next.'
> 2003: 'Think young. Drink young.'
> 2004: 'It's the cola.'"

Ries makes a convincing argument that *consistency* is key to the use of an effective tagline.

Chuck Ingersoll of Brandsandtags.com proposes these five guidelines for great taglines:[2]

1. A tagline is (and should be) *different than a byline*. JELL-O is the brand name. Pudding and pie filling is the byline. "There's always room for JELL-O" is the tagline.

2. A tagline should *communicate the unique essence and advantage of your brand*—not a whole bunch of things you believe you do well.

3. Make sure your tagline is *congruent with who you are*. If you tell people one thing but turn out to be another, you instantly lose credibility.

4. Your tagline should be *clear,* not necessarily clever. Crisp, descriptive, on-target, and benefit-oriented.

5. *Using or modifying an idiom can make your tagline even more memorable.* "Straighten up and dry right" for a hair straightening iron is "stickier" than "Gives you straight hair."

This last guideline, regarding the degree to which the tagline is *memorable*, can be particularly challenging to marketers.

Timothy R.V. Foster, the brains behind SloganMaker (www.adslogans.co.uk), argued that:[3]

---

[1] Ries, A. (2008, November 5). "What Marketers Can Learn From Obama's Campaign," *Advertising Age*.
[2] Ingersoll, C. (2008). "5 Guidelines for Great Taglines." Retrieved November 14, 2008, from Differentiate Yourself with a Tagline, Slogan or Name That Communicates Your Brand Essence: www.brandsandtags.com.

Memorability has to do with the ability the line has to be recalled unaided. A lot of this is based on the brand heritage and how much the line has been used over the years (consistency). But if it is a new line, what makes it memorable? I suggest that it is the story that is told in the advertisement—the big idea. In addition to a provocative…story, (1) alliteration, (2) coined words, and (3) puns are good ways of making a line memorable.

1. As an illustration of the effectiveness of *alliteration*, Foster used Jaguar's tagline "Don't dream it. Drive it," and Girl Guides' (UK) tagline "Dream. Dare. Do."

2. As an illustration of *coined words*, Foster used Burton Menswear's tagline "Everwear," and KP Peanuts' tagline "Pure Snacking. Pure snactivity."

3. As an illustration of *puns*, Foster used Finish Detergent's tagline "Brilliant cleaning starts with Finish," and Weight Watchers Frozen Meals' tagline "Taste. Not waist." and another that we saw in the matching exercise: "Nothing runs like a Deere."

Bill Schley, in *Why Johnny Can't Brand*[4] bemoans the state of current tagline creation, and remembers a time when the great marketing masters created winning taglines. "In the hands of the Titans, a tagline was designed to be a precision-cut selling gem, the catalyst for your entire Dominant Selling Idea, infusing your name and logo with instant selling power on sight. A tagline was your Dominant Selling Idea gift-wrapped in a magic word package, signed, sealed, and delivered to your mental doorstep." An excerpt from Schley's guidelines for effective taglines appears below:

1. The "taglines must be short" mandate is a myth. Look at…FedEx's original "When it absolutely positively has to be there overnight." Or Vicks Nyquil's "the nighttime, sniffling, sneezing, coughing, aching, stuffy head, fever so you can rest medicine."…If you can say it in two or three words, say it. But what's important is that it works, not that it works in three words or less.

2. Rhyming and other tenets from eighth-grade poetry class are good. Some people stick up their noses at rhyming…but rhyming is a musical memory trick that's as old as time. Alliteration, consonance, and other simple poetry devices add up to smooth, satisfying feelings to the ear and tongue. People love them. We should all be so lucky to come up with…"Takes a licking and keeps on ticking" or "The whole TV scene in one magazine."

3. Putting your brand name in the (tagline) is not always required. It's a case-by-case judgment…For example, Visa doesn't require it. The line is simply locked under the logo: "It's everywhere you want to be."

---

[3] Foster, T.R.V. (2002). "The Art and Science of the Advertising Slogan." Retrieved October 7, 2004, from Adslogans.com: www.adslogans.co.uk.
[4] Schley, B. (2005). *Why Johnny Can't Brand*. London: Penguin Books Ltd.

Some good examples of *including your brand name* in the tagline appear in the matching exercise (e.g., "There's always room for JELL-O," "Wait till we get our Hanes on you," and "What happens in Vegas stays in Vegas") and also include "My goodness, my Guinness!" and "America runs on Dunkin'" (Dunkin' Donuts). If the tagline includes a *rhyme with the brand name*, this can be particularly effective. Some good examples of this include "Leggo my Eggo," "Flick your Bic," and "Get some Gianelli in your belly."

Task 2—Brainstorming a Tagline for a New Product

Your second task is to brainstorm a tagline for a new product, the "VibeAwake" while taking into account the suggestions regarding effective taglines that appear in this exercise. This ingenious new product is a mattress pad designed to serve as an alarm clock. Instead of waking the consumer up with a loud alarm, the mattress pad can be set to shake the consumer awake. VibeAwake's parent company, LinensOnly, is planning to roll this new product out in the summer months, as parents and students are purchasing supplies to take to university. When the product is initially introduced, they plan that the first big target customer group will be university students—especially first-year students—who will be sharing a room for the first time in their lives and are concerned about waking their roommate with a traditional alarm clock. The executives at LinensOnly plan that as the VibeAwake moves through its life cycle, they will target other major customer segments, such as the deaf community.

Once you have settled on a tagline, you must provide a rationale/explanation for the tagline that you have created, and that rationale should be stated in terms of the suggestions regarding effective taglines that appear in this exercise. In many instances, a very good tagline does not follow all, or even most, of the suggestions regarding effective taglines that appear here. In fact, you can probably find effective taglines in the matching part of this exercise that don't adhere to *any* of these suggestions. These suggestions are just that, *suggestions*. But please do the hard work of taking these suggestions into account as you brainstorm, and explaining in your rationale which suggestions you have (and haven't) chosen to follow and why.

1. Tagline:

2. Rationale/Explanation of Choice:

(Do your best here – international branding agencies regularly charge up to US$100,000 and more for the development of brand names, taglines, and/or logos. You may very well be honing a valuable skill!)

Memorable Taglines—Answer Key

There's always room for <u>JELL-O</u>.

The ultimate driving machine. <u>BMW</u>

Generation next. <u>Pepsi</u>

Wait till we get our <u>Hanes</u> on you.

Got <u>Milk</u>?

Takes a licking and keeps on ticking. <u>Timex</u>

Just do it. <u>Nike</u>

Like a rock. <u>Chevrolet</u>

Have it your way. <u>Burger King</u>

Because I'm worth it. <u>L'Oréal</u>

Don't leave home without it. <u>American Express</u>

You're in good hands. <u>Allstate Insurance</u>

Keeps on going and going...<u>Energizer batteries</u>

Nothing runs like a <u>Deere (John Deere tractors)</u>.

<u>Bounty</u>: the quicker picker-upper.

Melts in your mouth, not in your hands. <u>M&Ms</u>

Priceless. <u>MasterCard</u>

Expect more. Pay less. <u>Target</u>

Eat fresh. <u>Subway restaurants</u>

15 minutes could save you 15%. <u>GEICO Insurance</u>

Once you pop, you can't stop. <u>Pringles</u>

What happens in <u>Vegas</u> stays in <u>Vegas (Las Vegas)</u>.

9. Memory Models and Promotional Strategies

Frazer Enterprises Inc. is a large conglomerate specializing in consumer goods such as food items and personal hygiene products. Frazer Inc. has recently developed a truly innovative, "new to the world" product: hard candies designed to replenish the important nutrients lost during strenuous exercise. The tentative, or working, name for this new item is Replenish.

Quali-Investigations Inc. is a market research firm specializing in qualitative consumer research. Frazer Enterprises and Quali-Investigations have enjoyed a long and productive relationship, and Quali-Investigations has played a pivotal role in assessing the potential market for this new product and researching consumer response to the Replenish product concept. A researcher at Quali-Investigations, Joanna Lopez, has been especially involved in the new product development process of the Replenish product.

Susan Stevens is the Product Category Manager at Frazer Inc. who will be responsible for the introduction of Replenish to the marketplace. Susan has set up a preliminary meeting with the advertising agency used by Frazer Inc. to discuss advertising strategies for the introduction of the Replenish product. However, before meeting with the advertising people, she wants to touch base once again with the researchers at Quali-Investigations. Susan has worked closely with the primary Quali-Investigations researcher on this project, Joanna "Jo" Lopez, during the new product development phase of the project. She trusts her knowledge of the targeted consumers and intends to use this knowledge as a resource in developing advertising strategies. She has asked Jo to meet with her to briefly discuss these issues.

The Meeting

Susan: "Hi, Jo. Good to see you again. Thanks for setting up this meeting on such short notice. I wanted to talk with you once more about introduction strategies for the Replenish product before I meet with the advertising people next week."

Jo: "No problem—have a seat, Susan. Knowing that you were coming in, I have actually been thinking about this for most of the morning. I feel strongly that the initial advertising for the Replenish product is crucial to the long-term success of the product, and I'm pleased that you're looking for our ideas on this. As I have been thinking, I keep coming back to the idea of consumers' memory processes."

Susan: "I don't understand—what does memory have to do with this? This is a brand new product—customers don't even know that the product exists yet. How could memory have anything to do with it?"

Jo: "Well, let's talk about that. Most models of memory propose that there exist three different types of memory systems: Sensory Memory, Short-Term Memory, and Long-Term Memory. However, calling each of them a type of 'memory' is actually a little bit confusing, because the first two don't have much to do with how we use the word 'memory' in everyday language.

"The first type, Sensory Memory, really has more to do with perception—how we bring in information and stimuli from the outside world through our five senses. It specifically addresses the exposure and attentional facets of perception. Sensory Memory has to do with how we bring outside stimuli and information in, and whether or not we pay further attention to it.

"The second type, Short-Term Memory, has everything to do with interpretation, comprehension, and learning. This type of memory is also often called 'working memory' because it is where we do all the hard work of attaching meaning to a stimulus.

"The third type of memory, Long-Term Memory, is what we usually mean when we use the word 'memory' in everyday language. It has to do with storing and retaining information for later use.

"So most memory models should probably more accurately be called information processing models, since they address a wide spectrum of processing: the perception of information, attaching meaning to information, and retaining information. In this way, perception, learning, and memory are all seen as part of the same process.

"In the model we're discussing, the Sensory Memory system is responsible for the initial—almost instantaneous—perception of an outside stimulus. Of course, no one can perceive all the multitude of stimuli that surround us at any one time. Whether or not a particular stimulus is attended to by a particular consumer has a lot to do with the needs and characteristics of that particular consumer, but can also be affected by 'stimulus factors.' This means that, in an advertising context, advertisers can build certain things into an ad that almost automatically trigger attention in the audience. These things that trigger attention can be related to the intensity of the stimulus. For instance, in most cases a loud stimulus is more likely to be perceived by Sensory Memory than a softer one, and large stimuli are more likely to be noticed than small stimuli. Color can also serve as a great attention-getter, with bright yellow and red typically attracting the most attention. The element of surprise or novelty is another way of triggering this automatic attention; if consumers are surprised by something, they tend to pay automatic attention to it. Just like our ancestors, if something surprises us, we must instantaneously assess whether it poses a threat to us.

"This automatic attention is not really a means of processing the outside stimuli, and in fact some theorists call it 'preprocessing.' But it is a means of choosing which of the multitude of stimuli that we are exposed to and should be attended to more carefully and therefore sent on to Short-Term Memory for processing. Because of this filter-like role, advertisers often pay special attention to Sensory Memory. They find ways to use stimulus factors like bright colors, loud noises, and the element of surprise to increase the chances that consumers will respond with automatic attention to the ad and send it through the attentional gate to Short-Term Memory.

"If Sensory Memory perceives a stimulus and sends it along to Short-Term Memory, the real processing of the incoming information begins. It is in Short-Term Memory that an effort is made to comprehend or make sense of the stimulus. However, Short-Term Memory is limited in its capacity. It's believed that only a few pieces of information can be processed at any one time, and that if information is not processed and sent along to Long-Term Memory within about 30 seconds or so, it is lost from the system altogether. Short-Term Memory is responsible for what is known as the *encoding* process, and it is through this encoding process that information is sent along and stored in Long-Term Memory.

"This encoding of information might be accomplished in a very shallow fashion—for instance, a consumer might repeat a catchy phrase over and over again to themselves, thereby committing the phrase to memory. But by far the most common way to encode new information is to 'link' it to knowledge structures that already exist in memory. That is, the consumer relates new information to old information in order to make sense of the new information. As you might imagine, this poses distinct difficulties when the stimulus is entirely new—for example, when the stimulus is a truly innovative new product, consumers may have difficulty determining what existing knowledge structures to relate it to. But assuming that the encoding process is successful, the information can then be placed in Long-Term Memory.

"So the primary function of Short-Term Memory is to link incoming information with knowledge structures that already exist in Long-Term Memory. Therefore, the relationship between Short-Term Memory and Long-Term Memory is a very strong one; in some models, they are almost indistinguishable. Whereas Sensory Memory can be seen as 'feeding into' Short-Term Memory in that the relationship is only one way, there is a constant back-and-forth between Short-Term Memory and Long-Term Memory. Short-Term Memory takes information (that it has been 'fed' by Sensory Memory) and links it to preexisting knowledge structures in Long-Term Memory. In order to do this, it must be able to scan and pull from Long-Term Memory the appropriate preexisting information. By linking the new information with the preexisting information and then placing this newly reorganized information back into Long-Term Memory, Short-Term Memory is constantly changing and reorganizing Long-Term Memory.

"In an advertising context, this encoding process is extremely important. Marketers try to encourage the formation of specific associations by showing strong links between their brand and certain concepts. For instance, marketers of Dodge Ram trucks wanted to associate their trucks with the concept of 'toughness,' so they showed these trucks with high imagery visuals such as 'Rock Em Sock Em Robots.' To the average American baby boomer, these 'Rock Em Sock Em Robots' are the absolute epitome of toughness!

"Additionally, when a product is brand new, associations can also be effectively encouraged through the use of comparative advertising. These ads essentially tell the consumer: think of this new product in this way. For instance, if you were marketing a new cell/mobile phone service in the United States, you would probably not use advertising dollars to convey a long explanation of who you are and what you do.

Instead you would probably use comparative advertising that quickly conveys: 'We are just like Verizon and AT&T, but we are…(*fill in the blank: cheaper; with more coverage; with fewer drop-offs—however you want to differentiate your new product in this product category*).'

"Most memory theorists agree that once information is placed in Long-Term Memory, it remains there for a long time; hence the name 'long-term'! There are very few capacity limitations in Long-Term Memory. However, the existence of information in Long-Term Memory does not guarantee that the information can be easily accessed or retrieved. If the information went through a very elaborate encoding process while in Short-Term Memory—in other words, many different 'links' were formed with preexisting knowledge structures—then it's more likely that the piece of information can be easily accessed and retrieved later. And even in those cases where information encoding was minimal, retrieval 'cues' can be used to facilitate the subsequent retrieval of information from Long-Term Memory. These retrieval cues are typically words or images that help the consumer remember the 'link' or association that was formed during the encoding process in Short-Term Memory.

"So you see, Susan, if we allow an understanding of memory systems to inform our decisions regarding communications strategies, we stand a better chance of effectively introducing this new product to consumers and positioning it properly in the marketplace."

Susan: "I'm starting to see why we pay you guys so much money! Okay, I accept that an understanding of consumers' memory structures should guide our initial communications strategies for this product. Now let's shift gears a little and talk about what those strategies might be. As you know, the success of this new product is extremely important to senior management at Frazer. Do you have time to start brainstorming on this?"

Jo: "Let's order in some lunch and keep going; I think it's a good idea to kick around some ideas while these issues are fresh in our minds."

Susan: "Thanks—it's very important that I have some understanding of where I want to go with these introductory marketing communications strategies before I meet with the advertising people next week. As you can see, I've been jotting down questions throughout this meeting. Let's start by addressing each of these questions…

When you were explaining Sensory Memory, I got the impression that this first type of memory acts as a sort of gatekeeper—that some information is sent along to Short-Term Memory, but a great deal of incoming information is not. If this is the case, how do I increase the chances that *our* ads are taken in by Sensory Memory and passed along to Short-Term Memory? In other words, what sorts of things can I build into our specific advertisements that will boost the chances that target audience members will 'take in' the ad and send it along to Short-Term Memory for processing?

You said that when information is in Short-Term Memory, it must go through encoding in order to be passed along to Long-Term Memory. If not, it is quickly lost from Short-Term Memory. Are there elements of the advertising message that can be used to encourage this encoding, or the formation of associations with prior knowledge? As you know, it is extremely important to me and to others at Frazer Inc. that this new product be positioned as a health and fitness supplement, rather than as a candy or snack. We at Frazer are hoping to use the Replenish product to enter the booming health and fitness market. It seems to me that the initial encoding process will drive advertising receivers' perceptions of the Replenish product, and therefore determine the *positioning* of Replenish in the marketplace. In other words, the types of 'knowledge structures' that this new product is 'linked' to will drive whether the Replenish product is successfully positioned in the market. Are there specific advertising strategies that you can suggest that will encourage the typical consumer to 'link' this new product concept to health and fitness concepts and other health-related products already present in their Long-Term Memory?

From what you've said, I know that one of the most important factors contributing to consumers' ability to easily retrieve information from Long-Term Memory is the amount and quality of encoding that the information received while being processed in Short-Term Memory. I've already asked questions about how we might encourage proper encoding of our advertising message. This last question focuses on additional ways in which we might be able to facilitate the retrieval of our message from Long-Term Memory. Are there promotional strategies that can be used to facilitate later retrieval of our message? Most of our customers will purchase this new product at their supermarket or drugstore. What additional things can we do at the point of purchase that will help consumers retrieve the advertising message information from Long-Term Memory while they are making the purchase decision?

Please do/answer the following:

THE AD

1. Brainstorm with your teammates to develop a 30-second TV ad that will be used to introduce this new product to the marketplace. Specifically describe this ad, using a storyboard and/or a few paragraphs of text.

2. Regarding the ad that you have developed and described in question 1, what *specific* elements of this ad will *increase the chances that this ad will be attended to by Sensory Memory*, and therefore passed through the attentional gate?

3. Regarding the ad that you have developed and described in question 1, what *specific* elements of this ad will *encourage the formation of associations* between this new product and things already familiar to the consumer? What specific familiar things will the ad "link" the new Replenish product with?

POINT-OF-PURCHASE

4. Now that you have comprehensively described the ad and answered questions 2 and 3, please also address point-of-purchase issues. How might you *encourage customers' retrieval of the ad's information at the point-of-purchase* as they are making their in-store purchase decision?

SECTION IV:

CUSTOMER MOTIVATION AND PERSONALITY

10. The Great Debate

The relationship between consumer marketing activities and consumer culture has long been debated. Whereas some theorists maintain that marketing practices have a profound influence on cultural norms and values, other theorists believe that marketing practices are typically designed in response to preexisting cultural norms and values. For instance, whereas it could be argued that the drive for conspicuous consumption in our society is the result of the proliferation of marketing activities in that society, it might just as easily be argued that the proliferation of marketing activities in our society is a reflection of the drive for conspicuous consumption.

One such relationship that is commonly debated is the relationship between advertising and materialism. The empirical research to support a relationship between advertising and materialism has been scant. However, Lee and Sirgy (1995) point out that no potential cause of materialism has received more attention and criticism than advertising. They believe that even in the absence of empirical support, most researchers and commentators agree that advertising causes an increase in materialism. Pollay and Mittal (1993) investigated consumers' perceptions of the relationship between advertising and its effects, and found that consumers perceive advertising as fostering materialism. Pollay and Mittal agree with these consumer perceptions, and point to advertising's role as an important social phenomenon in its ability to model certain values such as materialism. Schroeder (1992) also sees advertising as a primary vehicle in the promotion of materialistic values, and others support this view.

On the other hand, Holbrook (1987) feels strongly that the assumed relationship between advertising and materialism is misleading. Schudsen (1991) while acknowledging that advertising is often attacked as the cause of materialism in our society, states that since America was materialist long before advertising held much visibility or importance in American cultural life, such attacks are misguided. Rudmin (1992) echoes this sentiment by pointing out that materialism was one of the most notable traits of American society in the early 19th century, long before the appearance of contemporary correlates of materialism (such as mass media advertising) now cited as its cause. These theorists would argue that advertising is a reflection of the cultural value of materialism, rather than its cause.

Just as others have investigated the potential relationship between violence in the media and the fostering of aggression in our society, consumer behaviorists must question the relationship between advertising and materialism. Whereas the true relationship between advertising and materialism may ultimately be unknowable, the relationship is certainly worthy of debate.

Debate Rules

Note that the following rules are not based on any formally accepted rules of debate. The rules are informal and are designed to allow class members to present a well-reasoned argument with minimal preparation. The debate resolution (see "Resolution" on the next page) is worded in such a way that students should be able to develop a defensible position, either "pro" or "con," without any prior research preparation. Students do not need any formal debating experience to participate.

The Resolution

Be it resolved that advertising in contemporary Western culture is a primary cause of materialism in contemporary Western society.

The Assignment of Roles and Responsibilities

The Official
One member of the class will volunteer for, or be assigned by the professor to, the role of Debate Official. This individual will have responsibility for enforcing the time limits and ensuring that the rules of the debate are upheld.

The Teams
Eight members of the class will volunteer for, or be assigned by the professor to, the roles of debate team members. Two teams of four will be formed.

The Jury
The remaining members of the class will act as members of the jury, deciding the winner of the debate. If the number of jury members is even, the professor will also act as a member of the jury, so that the number of jury members is always odd (and hence a tie is impossible).

The Procedure

Step 1: Determination of Proposition and Opposition Teams
A coin toss begins this process. The team that wins the coin toss is allowed to choose which side of the debate, proposition (affirmative) or opposition (negative), they wish to represent. The role of the proposition team is to convince the jury that the Resolution is true. The role of the opposition team is to convince the jury that the Resolution is false.

Step 2: Preparation
Each of the teams is allowed to confer and plan their strategy for *eight minutes*. During this time, team members should develop sound arguments supporting their case, and should also prepare themselves to refute the other team's likely arguments. In addition, team members should assign specific roles (first speaker, second speaker, rebuttal speaker, and researcher) to each of the four team members.

The team roles are defined as follows:

> **First Speaker for the Proposition**—this speaker must first restate the resolution, and then provide clear and well-reasoned arguments in support of the resolution.

First Speaker for the Opposition—this speaker's role is to convince the jury that the proposition team's arguments are flawed, and provide new arguments that dispute the resolution.

Second Speaker for the Proposition—this speaker's role is to continue the argument of the First Speaker for the Proposition, refute the arguments of the First Speaker for the Opposition, and if appropriate introduce new lines of argument in support of the resolution.

Second Speaker for the Opposition—this speaker's role is to continue the argument of the First Speaker for the Opposition, refute the arguments of the First and Second Speakers for the Proposition, and if appropriate introduce new lines of argument that dispute the resolution.

Rebuttal Speaker for the Opposition—this speaker's role is to reiterate the most important Opposition arguments in a concise and very persuasive manner. No *new* arguments or facts may be presented at this time, but the speaker may address any issues previously raised by either team.

Rebuttal Speaker for the Proposition—this speaker's role is to reiterate the most important Proposition arguments in a concise and very persuasive manner. No <u>new</u> arguments or facts may be presented at this time, but the speaker may address any issues previously raised by either team.

Researcher (one for each team)—the researcher for each team does not have a speaking role. The researchers take notes during the debate and then confer with their team members before the rebuttal, playing an active role in developing a concise and clear rebuttal speech.

Step 3: The Debate
Timeline, order of speakers and speaking times for the debate are as follows:

8 minutes: Preparation

3 minutes: First Speaker for the Proposition
3 minutes: First Speaker for the Opposition
2 minutes: Second Speaker for the Proposition
2 minutes: Second Speaker for the Opposition

4 minutes: A break in the debate so that teams may confer with their researcher and plan the rebuttal speech.

2 minutes: Rebuttal Speaker for the Opposition (note the reversal of order here)
2 minutes: Rebuttal Speaker for the Proposition

Step 4: The Vote
All members of the jury must vote for the team that they feel has made the more convincing arguments. Jury members must be careful not to let their personal views or beliefs regarding the Resolution bias their vote. They must vote for the team that set forth the most convincing arguments. No member of the jury is allowed to abstain. Since the number of jury members is always odd, a tie vote is impossible. The team with the most votes wins the debate.

References:

Holbrook, M. B. (1987). "Mirror, Mirror, on the Wall, What's Unfair in the Reflections on Advertising?" *Journal of Marketing*, 51, 95–103.

Lee, D. & Sirgy, M. J. (1995). "Determinants of Involvement in the Consumer/Marketing Life Domain in Relation to Quality of Life: A Theoretical Model and Research Agenda," *Proceedings of the Fifth Quality-Of-Life/Marketing Conference: Developments in Quality-Of-Life Studies in Marketing,* Vol. V, eds. H. Lee Meadow, M. Joseph Sirgy, and Don Rahtz, DeKalb, IL: Academy of Marketing Science, 13–18.

Pollay, R. W. & Mittal, B. (1993). "Here's the Beef: Factors, Determinants, and Segments in Consumer Criticism of Advertising," *Journal of Marketing*, 57, 99–114.

Rudmin, F. W. (1992). "Materialism and Militarism: De Tocqueville on America's Hopeless Hurry to Happiness," *Meaning, Measure, and Morality of Materialism*, eds. Floyd Rudmin and Marsha Richins, Provo, UT: The Association for Consumer Research, 110–112.

Schroeder, J. E. (1992). "Materialism and Modern Art," *Meaning, Measure, and Morality of Materialism*, eds. Floyd Rudmin and Marsha Richins, Provo, UT: The Association for Consumer Research, 10–13.

Schudsen, M. (1991). "Delectable Materialism: Were the Critics of Consumer Culture Wrong All Along?" *The American Prospect*, 5, 26–35.

11. Maslow's Need Hierarchy and Customer Motivation

Jean-Claude Neville is CEO of a bicycle manufacturing company, Jacques Neville, Inc., in a small town in France. He has been in the bicycle business his whole life, having inherited the company from his father, Jacques. A Neville bicycle is considered one of the best in the world, and the Neville Company's products sell for between US$2,000 (on the low end) to more than US$10,000 (on the high end). Jean-Claude is proud of the reputation for quality that Neville enjoys throughout Europe.

Recently, Jean-Claude has been thinking more and more about the American market. He has seen data that suggest that Americans are joining golf/country clubs less than their parents did, but that bicycle clubs are rapidly increasing in popularity. He knows that the baby boomer demographic in the United States represents huge potential. As the American baby boomers move into their retirement years, Jean-Claude sees real opportunity there.

Jean-Claude has watched as Harley-Davidson, one of the companies that he most admires, has built a customer base that is perhaps the most loyal in the world. He knows that a great deal of Harley-Davidson's success is related to the customer events, rallies, and clubs that they sponsor, and he sees other organizations throughout the world connecting with their customers in this same way. For example, the Chinese car manufacturer Geely Automobile Holdings sponsors owners' clubs, which have been very effective in building brand loyalty for their cars.

Jean-Claude is excited about the possibility of sponsoring bicycle clubs in the United States and potentially riding a wave of interest in cycling in that country. He sees these clubs as a way to connect with the U.S. consumer and build a loyal following, something that his company has not been able to accomplish in the United States to the extent that they have in Europe. However, he feels that he doesn't really understand the typical bicycle club member. The Neville Company has traditionally catered to the sport bicyclist. Being a competitive cyclist himself, Jean-Claude certainly understands one's motivation to compete in this sport. But the motivation behind joining a cycling club is not something that he fully comprehends. Why are bicycle clubs growing in popularity in the United States? What *motivates* an American baby boomer to join one of these clubs?

As Jean-Claude pondered this question, he remembered a theory that he studied in university years ago: Maslow's Need Hierarchy.[1] He remembered this theory as being an overarching model of human needs, and he knows that, according to this theory, all human motivation stems from the drive to fulfill a need. He has no idea why this particular theory has stuck with him over the years, but he sent a quick mental "thank you" to his father, who pushed him to get a degree before taking over the family business.

Jean-Claude plugged "Maslow's Need Hierarchy" into his search engine, and the model appeared on his computer monitor just as he remembered it:

---

[1] Maslow, A. H. (1943). "A Theory of Human Motivation," *Psychological Review*, 370–396.

Jean-Claude refamiliarized himself with the model by reading the first few links that came up after his search engine inquiry, and he was pleased to find that he recognized most of the main tenets of the model. He remembered that the theory asserts that humans are motivated by unfulfilled needs, and that one or another level of need may be present at any time. Only when lower needs (on the hierarchy) are satisfied can one move up to focus on the next level of need. For example, if one is experiencing concerns related to safety needs, one must satisfy those needs before addressing needs related to belongingness. He understood the needs as follows:

- *Physiological Needs:* These needs encompass those things that humans need to survive, and may include anything that helps an individual stay alive. Things like food and water are often cited as satisfying physiological needs.

- *Safety Needs:* These needs encompass issues related to safety and security, and may include anything that helps the individual be free from the threat of physical and emotional harm.

- *Social/Belongingness Needs:* These needs have to do with humans' need to interact with other people, and may include the needs for love and friendship.

- *Esteem Needs:* These needs involve respect and recognition, and encompass both the need for self-respect, as well as the need for respect and recognition from others.

- *Self-Actualization Needs:* These needs represent the highest level of human functioning. The need for self-actualization involves the need to be the best that one can be. People who are focused on this need often talk of a need for enriching experiences.

Jean-Claude was still not convinced that this model would help him understand the motivations behind being a member of a bicycle club, but given the potential for sales growth in the United States, he decided to look into the matter further. The Neville Company had contracted with an international market research company, The UncoverInsights Group, in the past, and Jean-Claude decided to engage them once again to investigate American baby boomers and U.S. bicycle clubs. He directed The UncoverInsights Group to begin conducting focus groups among current bicycle club members in the United States who fit the baby boomer demographic. He noted that the planned discussion questions should revolve around those consumers' motivations for becoming members of the bicycle club to which they belonged.

Two weeks later, the transcript of the first focus group appeared in his e-mail, and he smiled as he began to read it. He didn't have to read very far into the transcript to find ample evidence that Maslow's theory had some application to this particular situation. In fact, he found an example of each of the five different types of hierarchical needs within the very first page of the transcript.

Please read each of the following excerpts from the focus group transcript and match that excerpt to one of the hierarchical needs identified in Maslow's Need Hierarchy. All of the five hierarchical needs are represented once.

Each of the following comments was made in response to the question, "Why did you join this bicycle club?"

Maya J. "I find that I learn so much from the others in the club. It is really important to me to keep learning and growing in all parts of my life—including cycling."

Need level: _____

Chuck S. "I had a heart attack a few years ago, and I was told by my doctors that I really needed to step up the amount of exercise that I get—my life depends on this club!"

Need level: _____

Eric P. "I have been cycling a long time, and I have become quite accomplished at it. I wanted to be around other people who could fully appreciate my skill level."

Need level: _____

Carolyn L. "I heard about this club and thought that it would be a great way to meet people."

Need level: _____

Dennis T. "I used to bike alone, but I had too many close calls, where a driver didn't see me and almost hit me. I decided that it would be smarter to join a club so that I would be cycling in a large group and be more visible."

     Need level: _____

After reading the entire focus group transcript and chatting with the focus group moderator about her impressions, Jean-Claude felt much better prepared to begin to explore the myriad of reasons why an American baby boomer might join a bicycle club.

12. Appealing to the Id, Superego, and Ego

Freud's Psychoanalytic Theory of Personality posits that there exist three parts of the human psyche: the id, the superego, and the ego. Theoretically, there is constant interaction between the id, the superego, and the ego, and the ways in which conflicts among these three elements are resolved, both on the conscious and the unconscious levels, will determine one's personality.

The three elements may be defined as follows:

> **The Id** represents the desire to gratify one's most primal and instinctive needs, regardless of the consequences. Its only concern is the avoidance of pain and the pursuit of pleasure.

> **The Superego** represents the internalization of society's ethical mores and moral standards. It has been characterized as the "conscience" of the psyche, since its focus is on good and upright behavior.

> **The Ego** is that part of the human psyche that seeks to balance the urges and impulses of the id with the honorable behavior dictated by the superego, and do so in a way which meets the needs of both.

Please do the following:

You are to brainstorm advertising ideas for a chocolate pudding powdered mix (adding milk to the mix produces chocolate pudding). Assume that the primary target market for this product is adult women, and that the ads will run in magazines. Develop three different print ads. The first ad will specifically appeal to the id, the second ad will specifically appeal to the superego, and the third ad will specifically appeal to the ego. Sketch out the ads (stick figures, etc., work fine here), and write at least one sentence under each ad, explaining its primary strategy.

SECTION V:
SEGMENTING, TARGETING, AND POSITIONING

13. VALS™ Segmentation Categories

VALS™ is the name of a widely used consumer categorization system developed by SRI International, and now owned by SRI Consulting Business Intelligence (SRIC-BI). The VALS system is a consumer psychographic segmentation system that places consumers into one of eight categories based on their answers to the VALS survey. This survey measures consumer resources as well as the underlying psychological motivations that many consumers share and that predict each group's typical choices as consumers.

The three *Primary Motivations* used to categorize consumers into the eight groups are ideals, achievement, and self-expression. As noted on the VALS website, "Consumers who are primarily motivated by **ideals** are guided by knowledge and principles. Consumers who are primarily motivated by **achievement** look for products and services that demonstrate success to their peers. Consumers who are primarily motivated by **self-expression** desire social or physical activity, variety, and risk." *Resources* include all assets that a consumer might have, including such things as financial assets, education, and energy. As noted on the website, "A person's tendency to consume goods and services extends beyond age, income, and education. Energy, self-confidence, intellectualism, novelty seeking, innovativeness, impulsiveness, leadership, and vanity play a critical role. These personality traits in conjunction with key demographics determine an individual's resources."

SRIC-BI has developed VALS systems for the United States, Japan, and the UK. The categories of the U.S. system, as shown and described on SRI's website (www.sric-bi.com/VALS) follow.

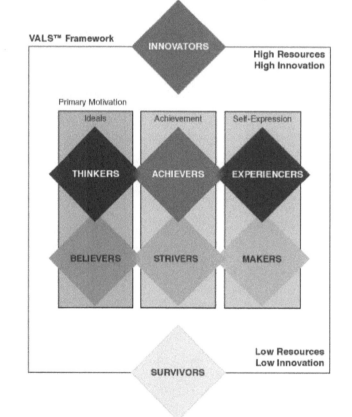

Source: SRI Consulting Business Intelligence (SRIC-BI); www.sric-bi.com/VALS.

Innovators

Innovators are successful, sophisticated, take-charge people with high self-esteem. Because they have such abundant resources, they exhibit all three primary motivations in varying degrees. They are change leaders and are the most receptive to new ideas and technologies. Innovators are very active consumers, and their purchases reflect cultivated tastes for upscale, niche products and services.

Image is important to Innovators, not as evidence of status or power but as an expression of their taste, independence, and personality. Innovators are among the established and emerging leaders in business and government, yet they continue to seek challenges. Their lives are characterized by variety. Their possessions and recreation reflect a cultivated taste for the finer things in life.

Thinkers

Thinkers are motivated by ideals. They are mature, satisfied, comfortable, and reflective people who value order, knowledge, and responsibility. They tend to be well educated and actively seek out information in the decision-making process. They are well-informed about world and national events and are alert to opportunities to broaden their knowledge.

Thinkers have a moderate respect for the status quo institutions of authority and social decorum, but are open to consider new ideas. Although their incomes allow them many choices, Thinkers are conservative, practical consumers; they look for durability, functionality, and value in the products they buy.

Achievers

Motivated by the desire for achievement, Achievers have goal-oriented lifestyles and a deep commitment to career and family. Their social lives reflect this focus and are structured around family, their place of worship, and work. Achievers live conventional lives, are politically conservative, and respect authority and the status quo. They value consensus, predictability, and stability over risk, intimacy, and self-discovery.

With many wants and needs, Achievers are active in the consumer marketplace. Image is important to Achievers; they favor established, prestige products and services that demonstrate success to their peers. Because of their busy lives, they are often interested in a variety of time-saving devices.

Experiencers

Experiencers are motivated by self-expression. As young, enthusiastic, and impulsive consumers, Experiencers quickly become enthusiastic about new possibilities but are equally quick to cool. They seek variety and excitement, savoring the new, the offbeat, and the risky. Their energy finds an outlet in exercise, sports, outdoor recreation, and social activities.

Experiencers are avid consumers and spend a comparatively high proportion of their income on fashion, entertainment, and socializing. Their purchases reflect the emphasis they place on looking good and having "cool" stuff.

Believers

Like Thinkers, Believers are motivated by ideals. They are conservative, conventional people with concrete beliefs based on traditional, established codes: family, religion, community, and the nation. Many Believers express moral codes that are deeply rooted and literally interpreted. They follow established routines, organized in large part around home, family, community, and social or religious organizations to which they belong.

As consumers, Believers are predictable; they choose familiar products and established brands. They favor American products and are generally loyal customers.

Strivers

Strivers are trendy and fun loving. Because they are motivated by achievement, Strivers are concerned about the opinions and approval of others. Money defines success for Strivers, who don't have enough of it to meet their desires. They favor stylish products that emulate the purchases of people with greater material wealth. Many see themselves as having a job rather than a career, and a lack of skills and focus often prevents them from moving ahead.

Strivers are active consumers because shopping is both a social activity and an opportunity to demonstrate to peers their ability to buy. As consumers, they are as impulsive as their financial circumstance will allow.

Makers

Like Experiencers, Makers are motivated by self-expression. They express themselves and experience the world by working on it—building a house, raising children, fixing a car, or canning vegetables—and have enough skill and energy to carry out their projects successfully. Makers are practical people who have constructive skills and value self-sufficiency. They live within a traditional context of family, practical work, and physical recreation and have little interest in what lies outside that context.

Makers are suspicious of new ideas and large institutions such as big business. They are respectful of government authority and organized labor, but resentful of government intrusion on individual rights. They are unimpressed by material possessions other than those with a practical or functional purpose. Because they prefer value to luxury, they buy basic products.

Survivors

Survivors live narrowly focused lives. With few resources with which to cope, they often believe that the world is changing too quickly. They are comfortable with the familiar and are primarily concerned with safety and security. Because they must focus on meeting needs rather than fulfilling desires, Survivors do not show a strong primary motivation.

Survivors are cautious consumers. They represent a very modest market for most products and services. They are loyal to favorite brands, especially if they can purchase them at a discount.

Please do the following:

Each of the following eight paragraphs describes a consumer who might be seen as a "typical Joe" or "typical Jill" for a specific VALS™ category. Your task is to identify which VALS category is being described by placing the name of the VALS category in the blank space at the end of each paragraph. Note that all eight VALS categories are represented, and no VALS category appears more than once.

1. Jill is a retired English professor. She and her husband invested their money wisely while they were working, and they are enjoying a comfortable retirement. She likes to take educational tours for vacation, and continues to attend conferences, seminars, and other events that are consistent with her philosophy of life-long learning. She reads the *New York Times* faithfully and watches CNN every evening. With regard to purchases, Jill is relatively conventional. The products she buys are no-nonsense; no flamboyant, trendy products for her. She has a subscription to *Consumer Reports*, and uses this resource frequently so she can make informed consumer decisions.
VALS™ Category:_____

2. Jill lives with her husband and four children in a town not far from a National Forest. She and her husband love the outdoors and take their kids camping most summers so they will grow up to love the outdoors, too. She and her husband have a vegetable garden and raise chickens. Her husband is a carpenter and recently added on a family room to their home. With regard to purchases, she buys only what the family needs. She is a member of the local co-op, and tries to buy most of their necessary goods there.
VALS™ Category:_____

3. Joe plays checkers in the park each day at the same time with the same people. He walks there every morning from his small one-room apartment three blocks away. He has been retired for 10 years now, and before that he worked as a laborer for the city. He has no savings, and his social security and small pension check just barely cover his rent, food, and medications. With regard to purchases, Joe is extremely careful. Because of his very limited funds he must worry about even the smallest of purchases.
VALS™ Category:_____

4. Jill is a bioengineer with a new start-up firm. She is young, unmarried, and very active. She is an energetic rock-climber and skier, and is training for her first marathon. She has a large social circle, and is always looking forward to the next social activity or event. In the evenings, she is frequently at clubs with her friends, and the clubs she patronizes change from month to month as new ones becomes "hot." With regard to purchases, she typically goes for very new

and different styles. However, as soon as the style becomes more mainstream, she abandons it for the next new trend.
VALS™ Category:_____

5. Jill is the CEO of her company. She also has a law degree. She enjoys being in charge of the company and hopes her example will inspire young women to strive for top leadership positions in business. She serves on the boards of a number of other firms, and is very active with local nonprofit agencies. She loves live theater and usually buys season tickets. With regard to purchases, Jill has extremely discriminating tastes. In terms of fashion, she has an artistic flair and seems to know immediately whether something is "her" or not. She loves her iPhone and in-car GPS system. Recently, she hired a consultant to recommend ways to make her business more sustainable.
VALS™ Category:_____

6. Joe is a member of the military, and has been for nearly 18 years. He and his wife have three children, and frequently move from base to base as his assignment changes. He takes the saying "Duty, Honor, Country" very seriously, and he is an active member of the Baptist faith. When he is reassigned to a new base, the first thing he and his wife do is seek out others who share their faith; they find that this is the fastest way to feel like part of the new community. His purchasing patterns are fairly routine, and he buys as much as possible at the military base. His income is limited, and so he tries to stay with products that he knows and trusts.
VALS™ Category:_____

7. Joe is a financial manager working in a large corporation. He has been working for this firm for the past 15 years, and is on track to meet his goal of being a member of senior management by the time he is 45. His wife works in the marketing department of the same firm. He is pursuing his MBA in the evenings at the local university. They have two young kids and live in the suburbs. Between work, the MBA, and kids, neither Joe nor his wife have much time for personal hobbies. With regard to purchases, Joe almost always buys recognized brands. He wishes he didn't have to use his credit card so much, but it's a trade-off he feels is worth it. He feels that the car he drives, the shoes he wears, and the home he owns are well-deserved rewards for his hard work.
VALS™ Category:_____

8. Joe has an associate's degree from the local community college, and has had an entry-level job at one of the large manufacturing companies in town for many years. Although his boss has encouraged him to continue his education and pursue a bachelor's degree, he never seems to have the time. He is young and unmarried and lives in a small apartment. He has expensive tastes in cars, and pays more in car payments each month than he does in rent. With regard to purchases, Joe tends to be a trend-watcher. He likes nice things, and always seems to spend more than he can afford.
VALS™ Category:_____

14. Positioning Strategies

Positioning is all about how a company wants its target consumers to *perceive* its product or service. In many cases, a company can choose from a number of different positioning strategies.

These positioning strategies may include:

1. *Positioning by attribute*—associating a product with a particular feature.
2. *Positioning by benefit*—associating a product with a customer benefit.
3. *Positioning by use*—associating a product with a specific use or application.
4. *Positioning by user*—associating a product with a user or group of users.
5. *Positioning by competitor*—differentiating a product from a competitor's product.
6. *Positioning by product category*—associating a product with others in a similar product category, or conveying how it differs from all others in that category.

Part 1

Please do the following:

Listed below are examples of seven different positioning strategies that might be used with high-end sunglasses. Your task is to identify which positioning strategy is being used in each example. Do this by placing the number of the positioning strategy (see above) in the blank space after each of the seven examples. Note that all positioning strategies are represented, and no positioning strategy appears more than once.

"The sunglasses for the discriminating buyer" _____

"These sunglasses block more harmful rays than Brand *X*." _____

"The sunglasses with unbreakable lenses." _____

"The best sunglasses for sports activities." _____

"These sunglasses reduce glare in order to provide you with clear vision." _____

"The sunglasses that are a fashion statement, rather than a fashion accessory." _____

Part 2

Please do the following:

Now that you have some experience with these different positioning strategies, try coming up with some of your own. For each of the following positioning strategies, come up with an example of how that strategy might be used to position a deodorant/antiperspirant.

1. Positioning by attribute:

2. Positioning by benefit:

3. Positioning by use:

4. Positioning by user:

5. Positioning by competitor:

6. Positioning by product category:

15. Adopter Categories

In its Annual Design Awards 2004, *BusinessWeek* highlighted the very prolific new product idea generators at Nike. Giving Nike a bronze award that year, writers at *BusinessWeek* pointed out that Nike researchers came up with no fewer than 33 high performance golf tee new product concepts! These ideas included: "tees made of fertilizer; tees that fit in a wallet; tees that disintegrate on impact; and the Mojo, a tee with a liquid center containing Tiger Woods' sweat (remember, it's just a concept)."[1]

Let's enter the hypothetical world of Mike (pronounced, in this case, my-kee), where one of these new product concepts—*the golf tee made of fertilizer*—has just been picked up, and you are assigned to run with it. The target market for this new product includes all golfers. You have outsourced some of the branding work, and a contract branding firm is currently in the process of developing name and tagline proposals for this new product. However, your chief marketing officer (CMO) is extremely sensitive to time-to-market metrics—the time it takes from first picking up a new product idea until commercialization—and so she is pushing you to develop a comprehensive marketing plan even before the name of the product has been established. She is especially interested in the long-term sales prospects of this product, since she has been disappointed lately by new products that had very good short-term sales, but were not able to produce revenues over the long haul.

Your CMO has asked you to take a look at the adopter categories for this new product and come up with relevant promotional campaign ideas for each category. By assessing all of the different adopter categories for this new product, she can be sure that every stage of the life cycle of this new product has been taken into account. In her opinion, too many brand managers take a short-term view and only plan for the Introduction and Growth stages of a new product's life cycle.

So, in the interests of a comprehensive, long-term marketing plan for this ingenious new golf tee made of fertilizer, you are currently involved in creating promotional campaigns targeted toward each of the five categories of new product adopters: Innovators, Early Adopters, Early Majority, Late Majority, and Laggards. As you know, these categories are, in essence, customer segments. Back in the 1950s, Everett Rogers created a model[2] that classifies the universe of all customers who will eventually adopt a new product into five segments according to the length of time that it takes them to adopt the innovation.

Much has been written about these five adopter categories. Many descriptions of the categories point out the demographic differences that are typically found among them. For instance, as one moves from those who are quickest to adopt a new product to those who are slowest (i.e., from Innovators to Laggards) income levels typically decrease, and average age typically increases. Just as interesting, however, are the psychographic descriptions that have been proposed for these five customer segments. The psychographic descriptions are especially helpful in understanding what motivates the product adoption of each group of customers, and are therefore

---

[1] *BusinessWeek.* (2004, July 5). "Annual Design Awards," *BusinessWeek*, p. 68.
[2] Rogers, E. M. (1955). *Diffusion of Innovation.* New York: Free Press.

extremely valuable in pointing to the differing promotional messages that may resonate with each group.

Innovators (approximately 2.5% of all adopters)

This small group includes the consumers who are the very first to adopt a new product. These consumers are typically extremely involved in the overall product category of the new product. Because these consumers are intensely involved in the product category, and typically read everything they can about the industry, they are often aware that a new product is coming out even before it is commercialized. These consumers have a great base of knowledge about your product category.

Given their intense involvement with the product category and their wide-ranging knowledge base in that category, Innovators are usually open to receiving a lot of information about the new product. The Innovator's motivation to adopt a new product typically stems from the gratifying personal experience they expect to have with the new product, and their motivation to learn more about the newest product in a product category.

Early Adopters (approximately 13.5% of all adopters)

These consumers are the second group to adopt a new product. Given how small the Innovator group is, this group represents the first moderately sized group of consumers to adopt the new product. These consumers are typically more socially involved in local groups than the Innovators, and so they are often important trendsetters and opinion leaders in the product category.

The Early Adopter's motivation to adopt a new product typically stems from the pride that they derive from their role as an opinion leader. They get satisfaction and status from being the first in their social community to adopt a new product, and they enjoy being seen by others as a trendsetter in that product category.

Early Majority (approximately 34% of all adopters)

Members of the Early Majority make up approximately one-third of all adopters. Of the two categories that make up the bulk of all new product adopters, the Early Majority and the Late Majority, members of this Early Majority are on the front end of the adoption process. However, they are typically more cautious than the Innovator and Early Adopter consumers, and this leads them to look outside of themselves for guidance in their adoption decisions.

Early Majority consumers' adoption processes tend to be motivated by seeing others' use of the product, especially if someone that they admire is depicted as having a positive experience with the new product.

Late Majority (approximately 34% of all adopters)

Like the members of the Early Majority, members of the Late Majority make up approximately one-third of all consumers. However, these members are further along on the timeline of adoption. By the time that consumers in the Late Majority group are considering the new product, it is typically not very new anymore. But it seems new to them, and this newness is somewhat threatening to these consumers. The word most often associated with members of the Late Majority is "skeptical." These consumers are not only cautious, but also distrusting of new products and any claims made about them.

Members of the Late Majority often look for reassurance in order to lessen their discomfort with new products. The adoption process of these consumers can be motivated by marketers' attempts to establish credibility for the new product and decrease the perceived threat associated with it. Promises of things like a "*Good Housekeeping*® seal of approval," or reassurances like "nine out of ten doctors agree…" often work well here.

Laggards (approximately 16% of all adopters)

The consumers in the Laggards category are the very last 16% of consumers to adopt a new product. They are very tradition bound, and resist adopting a new product until they no longer see it as being a "new" product. In other words, Laggards typically only surrender and adopt a new product when they perceive it as being part of the mainstream in that product category.

Typically, a Laggard's adoption of a new product is motivated by the perception that the new product represents what is now the established and conventional product in that product category. In other words, once they perceive the new product as being *not* new, they will consider adopting it.

Now, during these initial planning stages for the new fertilizer tee, your CMO has asked you to prepare a brief report that articulates the persuasive messages that you plan to use with each of these five different adopter categories. Specifically, she has asked that you describe how you will persuade each group of consumers to adopt this new product, and she has asked that you not use more than three sentences per description.

1. We will persuade the Innovators to adopt this new product by focusing our persuasive message on…

2. We will persuade the Early Adopters to adopt this new product by focusing our persuasive message on…

3. We will persuade the Early Majority consumers to adopt this new product by focusing our persuasive message on…

4. We will persuade the Late Majority consumers to adopt this new product by focusing our persuasive message on…

5. We will persuade the Laggards to adopt this new product by focusing our persuasive message on…

SECTION VI:

REFERENCE GROUP INFLUENCE AND DIFFUSION OF INNOVATIONS

16. Forms of Reference Group Influence

A reference group can be defined as a group or individual (i.e., opinion leader) having significant relevance upon one's evaluations, aspirations, and/or behavior. There are a number of ways in which reference persons and groups may influence a consumer. Those who study the question, "Why are we influenced by others?" have identified five types of *Social Power*:[1]

- **Reward Power**: Influence due to a reference group/individual's ability to dispense rewards.

- **Coercive Power**: Influence due to a reference group/individual's ability to administer punishment.

- **Referent Power**: Influence due to the influenced person's desire to identify with someone or to be like them.

- **Expert/Information Power**: Influence due to the influenced person's tendency to heed expert advice, or to listen to those who have information that one does not.

- **Legitimate Power**: Influence due to the influenced person's feelings of obligation.[2]

These different types of Social Power can, through various forms of reference group influence, lead to different levels of *Influence Results*:

- **Compliance**: Going along with group/individual norms to obtain approval or avoid disapproval.

- **Identification**: Going along with a group/individual in order to create or maintain a rewarding self-defining relationship with that group/individual.

- **Internalization**: Accepting group/individual norms and values as one's own.

Below, please note the relationships between *Types of Social Power* (1), *Forms of Reference Group Influence* (2), and different *Influence Results* (3):

1. Reward and Coercive Power → 2. Normative/Utilitarian Influence → 3. Compliance

1. Referent Power → 2. Value-Expressive Influence → 3. Identification

1. Expert/Information Power → 2. Informational Influence → 3. Internalization

---

[1] For instance, French, J. J., & Raven, B. (1959). "The Bases of Social Power." In D. Cartwright, *Studies in Social Power* (pp. 150–167). Ann Arbor, MI: Institute for Social Research.

[2] Legitimate Power is the least often viewed in a marketing context, and will not be discussed further.

As can be seen in the relationships on the previous page, *Forms of Reference Group Influence* are typically classified into three types:

- **Normative/Utilitarian** (related to *Reward* and *Coercive* forms of social power and resulting in *Compliance*)

  This type of influence derives from the reference person or group's ability to reward or punish the consumer. These rewards and punishments may be social in nature, as in the dispensing of social approval and disapproval.

- **Value-Expressive** (related to the *Referent* form of social power and resulting in *Identification*)

  This type of influence derives from the consumer's wish to identify with, or feel similar to, the reference person or group. The consumer experiences enhanced self-esteem through his/her emulation of the reference group's values and behaviors.

- **Informational** (related to the *Expert/Information* form of social power and resulting in *Internalization*)

  This type of influence derives from the reference person or group's possession of special knowledge or information that the consumer views as valuable. The consumer is influenced because he/she perceives the reference group's opinions and choices as being based on superior knowledge or experience.

Please do the following:

For each of the situations described below, identify which *Form of Reference Group Influence* is likely at work. Note: There are four of each of the three types of reference group influence represented here.

1. **While at summer camp, Rachel notices that all the members of an older "clique" that she admires eat granola bars at snack time. When she's back home again, she asks her mom to buy her some granola bars.**

   Form of Reference Group
   Influence (circle one):   *Normative/Util.*   (*Value-Expressive*)   *Informational*

2. **Ken sees a commercial in which a professional nutritionist explains the positive results of an adequate intake of vitamin D. Ken adds vitamin D to the list of nutritional supplements that he already takes.**

   Form of Reference Group
   Influence (circle one):   *Normative/Util.*   *Value-Expressive*   (*Informational*)

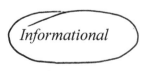

3. Pat's friends tease him about the old watch he's been wearing since high school. He decides it's finally time to buy a new watch.

Form of Reference Group
Influence (circle one):   (Normative/Util.)   *Value-Expressive*   *Informational*

4. Sheila is heading into her middle years, and decides that she needs to get more exercise. She joins a local softball league. She is surprised to learn that all the other women on her team are new to the sport, just like her, except for one woman who has played the sport for decades. This woman with experience uses a Louisville Slugger bat. When Sheila goes to buy her own bat, she chooses a Louisville Slugger.

Form of Reference Group
Influence (circle one):   *Normative/Util.*   *Value-Expressive*   (Informational)

5. Jason's favorite professional hockey player becomes a celebrity spokesperson for a specific brand of weed killer. Jason switches to that brand of weed killer.

Form of Reference Group
Influence (circle one):   *Normative/Util.*   (Value-Expressive)   *Informational*

6. Two coworkers comment to Jane that they really like the type of shoes she is wearing and ask her where she purchased them. The next time Jane needs shoes, she looks for the same brand.

Form of Reference Group
Influence (circle one):   (Normative/Util.)   *Value-Expressive*   *Informational*

7. Karen herself can't tell the difference between high-priced brands of wine and the more low-priced brands, so she usually purchases a cheap brand for her own use. However, when she is choosing a bottle of wine to take to a friend's house for dinner, she purchases a very expensive brand.

Form of Reference Group
Influence (circle one):   (Normative/Util.)   *Value-Expressive*   *Informational*

8. Michael has just taken his first job after graduating from college, and is looking forward to being a successful professional just like the men and women in his office that he admires. Although many different styles of dress are acceptable at his work, he notices that most of the male professionals in his office that he admires wear shirts with button-down collars. Michael buys a number of these shirts in several different colors.

Form of Reference Group
Influence (circle one):   *Normative/Util.*   (*Value-Expressive*)   *Informational*

9. Theresa has joined a new church and likes the people there very much. She notes that many of the other elderly women wear pantsuits to church. Although Theresa would be uncomfortable wearing pants to church, she does buy a few pantsuits to wear at home.

Form of Reference Group
Influence (circle one):   (*Normative/Util.*)   *Value-Expressive*   *Informational*

10. Mark's computer has crashed once again, and he decides that it's time to buy a new one. His sister, Sharon, is a computer engineer, so Mark phones Sharon to get some brand recommendations.

Form of Reference Group
Influence (circle one):   *Normative/Util.*   *Value-Expressive*   (*Informational*)

11. Fred sees an ad for soap that depicts someone being shunned by his friends because of bad body odor. The next time he's at the supermarket, Fred buys this brand of soap.

Form of Reference Group
Influence (circle one):   (*Normative/Util.*)   *Value-Expressive*   *Informational*

12. Susan notices that her auto mechanic drives a Honda automobile. She makes a mental note to include that brand in her search process the next time she's in the market for a new car.

Form of Reference Group
Influence (circle one):   *Normative/Util.*   *Value-Expressive*   (*Informational*)

17. Types of Reference Groups

Consumers typically belong to a myriad of different reference groups. We often classify these different reference groups into categories, using such criteria as whether the group is formal or informal and whether it is a membership or an aspirational group.

Formal vs. Informal—a formal reference group has a defined and documented structure, whereas an informal reference group possesses no defined structure. When informal roles exist within an informal group, they are never written.

Membership vs. Aspirational—membership reference groups are those groups to which the consumer belongs, whereas aspirational groups are those groups to which the consumer wishes to belong, but currently does not.

Please do the following:

For each of the four situations described next (each of these also appears in the "Forms of Reference Group Influence" case), identify which type of reference group is being described by circling the appropriate quadrant of the matrix. Note: each of the four types of reference groups appears once.

Two coworkers comment to Jane that they really like the type of shoes she is wearing and ask her where she purchased them. The next time Jane needs shoes, she looks for the same brand.

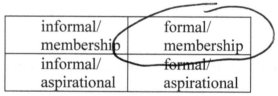

informal/ membership	formal/ membership
informal/ aspirational	formal/ aspirational

Karen herself can't tell the difference between high-priced brands of wine and the more low-priced brands, so she usually purchases a cheap brand for her own use. However, when she is choosing a bottle of wine to take to a friend's house for dinner, she purchases a very expensive brand.

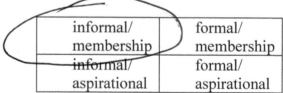

informal/ membership	formal/ membership
informal/ aspirational	formal/ aspirational

Michael has just taken his first job after graduating from college, and is looking forward to being a successful professional just like the men and women in his office that he admires. Although many different styles of dress are acceptable at his work, he notices that most of the male professionals in his office that he admires wear shirts with button-down collars. Michael buys a number of these shirts in several different colors.

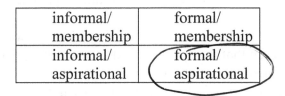

informal/ membership	formal/ membership
informal/ aspirational	(formal/ aspirational)

While at summer camp, Rachel notices that all the members of an older "clique" that she admires eat granola bars at snack time. When she's back home again, she asks her mom to buy her some granola bars.

informal/ membership	formal/ membership
(informal/ aspirational)	formal/ aspirational

18. Diffusion of Innovation

Diffusion of innovation refers to the process by which a new product spreads throughout a consumption population. Most marketers are very interested in achieving a quick rate of diffusion in order to shorten a new product's payback period and increase profitability.

Certainly, one of the most important factors influencing a new product's rate of diffusion is the extent to which that new product is discussed in a positive way among consumption population members. Therefore, marketers are very interested in understanding, and in many cases influencing, the "buzz" that is generated by the new product, both in terms of face-to-face and electronic word-of-mouth.

The "communicability/observability" of a new product has to do with the likelihood that members of a consumption population will be inclined to discuss the new product (personally and/or electronically), the ease with which the new product and its benefits can be communicated among these population members, and the degree to which the new product is likely to be observed in use.

Communicability/Observability is just one factor that influences the diffusion rate of innovations. A number of characteristics of an innovative new product will affect the rate with which customers adopt the innovation, and therefore, the speed with which the product/service will be diffused in the marketplace.

Five of these characteristics follow:

- **Communicability/Observability**: The probability that a new product will generate positive word-of-mouth, the ease with which the product's attributes and benefits can be communicated, and the social visibility of a new product.

- **Relative Advantage**: The degree to which consumers perceive the new product as being superior to existing alternatives.

- **Compatibility**: The extent to which the new product is perceived by consumers as consistent with their prior behaviors and values.

- **Complexity**: The degree to which the new product is difficult to understand and use.

- **Trialability**: The ease with which a new product can be sampled or tried on a limited basis (also sometimes called *Divisibility*).

Please do the following:

1. Choose any two products that you would consider relatively new to the marketplace. Write the new products you have chosen in the spaces provided on the next page.

2. For each new product, analyze the degree to which it possesses each of the listed characteristics (you must mark "high" or "low"), and predict how this can be expected to affect the diffusion rate of the new product (you must mark "Increase rate" or "Decrease rate").

New Product: _____

Characteristic			Influence on the Rate of Diffusion (check one)	
	High	Low	Increase Rate	Decrease Rate
Comm./Obs.				
Relative Advantage				
Compatibility				
Complexity				
Trialability				

New Product: _____

Characteristic			Influence on the Rate of Diffusion (check one)	
	High	Low	Increase Rate	Decrease Rate
Comm./Obs.				
Relative Advantage				
Compatibility				
Complexity				
Trialability				

SECTION VII:

CUSTOMER ATTITUDES

19. Hierarchies of Effects

The Hierarchies of Effects are based on the tri-component model of attitudes. The tri-component model of attitudes proposes that attitudes are composed of affect, behavior, and cognition—the "ABCs" of attitude structure:

- *Affect* involves the way a consumer *feels* about an attitude object;

- *Behavior* involves the person's behavior toward, or intentions to *do* something with regard to, an attitude object;

- *Cognition* involves the *beliefs* a consumer has about an attitude object.

These "ABC" (or "feel, do, believe") elements can be combined in different ways to create an attitude. The Hierarchies of Effects focus on the sequence of steps that occur. For example, if a consumer first constructs beliefs (cognition) about a product/service, then decides how she feels about it (affect), and then purchases it (behavior), she would be following the Standard Learning Hierarchy.

The *consistency principle* (discussed in more detail in the case "Balance Theory and Spokesperson Strategies") stresses that human beings are motivated to maintain consistency among their beliefs, emotions, and behaviors. In other words, the three components of attitude are unlikely to be at odds with one another. So if one component—say, for example, emotions—is predominant in the creation of an attitude, the other two components—in this case, behaviors and beliefs—are likely to follow along.

The sequences of elements that comprise the Hierarchies of Effects are displayed and described below.

The Standard Learning Hierarchy

Cognition → Affect → Behavior

In this hierarchy, the consumer approaches a product decision as a problem-solving process. The consumer first formulates relatively elaborate beliefs surrounding the product/service. Then, based on those beliefs, the consumer develops an emotional stance (or like/dislike) toward the product/service. Then, based on these beliefs and emotions, the consumer decides how to behave toward that product/service. In many cases, this behavior is a simple purchase/nonpurchase behavior, but behavior may also include finding out more about a product, trying the product on a limited basis, and other consumer actions related to the product/service.

The Low-Involvement Hierarchy

Cognition (minor) → Behavior → Affect

The Low-Involvement Hierarchy is similar to the Standard Learning Hierarchy in that the sequence begins with cognition. However, in the Standard Learning Hierarchy those cognitions are "relatively elaborate beliefs." In the Low-Involvement Hierarchy, these cognitions are very basic, and may involve mere brand familiarity or very general associations with a brand name. So, in this Low-Involvement Hierarchy, the consumer acts on very minor initial knowledge, often purchasing a product/service based on very limited beliefs. Only after the consumer has engaged in behavior toward the product/service (often a purchase/nonpurchase behavior) does the consumer attempt to evaluate like/dislike of the product/service.[1]

The Experiential Hierarchy

Affect → Behavior → Cognition

In this hierarchy, consumers act on the basis of their affective reactions to a product/service. They first respond to the product/service on an emotional level, and then act based on this affective response. Only after the consumer has engaged in behavior toward the product/service (often a purchase/nonpurchase behavior) does the consumer begin to formulate belief structures surrounding the product/service.[2]

Part 1

Next, three consumers, Terry M., Chris R., and Ashley S., have described their recent purchase of running shoes/sneakers. Brands X, Y, and Z are the primary competitors in this product space.

Please place the name of the Hierarchy of Effects that the consumer likely used in the space following each consumer's quote.

> **Terry M. purchased Brand X running shoes:** "I had to go to the shoe store with my daughter to buy some back-to-school shoes, and I knew that I needed some sneakers to replace my old ones. I was aware that I'd seen advertising for brands X and Z, and of those two whose advertising I'd seen, only brand X was running a sale on that day. So I purchased Brand X, and I've really come to like them."

Hierarchy of Effects likely utilized by Terry M.: *LOW-INVOLVEMENT HIERARCHY*

---

[1] Some theorists maintain that this after-the-fact evaluation may not occur at all in a very Low-Involvement situation, making the hierarchy appear simply: Cognition (minor) → Behavior.

[2] Some theorists maintain that this after-the-fact formulation of beliefs may not occur at all in an Experiential Hierarchy, making the hierarchy appear simply: Affect → Behavior.

Chris R. purchased Brand Y running shoes: "I was wandering around the mall with my girlfriends last week. We went by a shoe store—I can't even remember which store it was—and I saw these sneakers in the window. Honestly, they were just calling to me! Aren't they gorgeous?" (she holds her feet up) "Now that I have them, I just wear them everywhere! And I've found that they're actually really very comfortable."

Hierarchy of Effects likely utilized by Chris R.: *THE EXPERIMENTAL HIERARCHY*

Ashley S. purchased Brand Z running shoes: "I looked online and used the information there to compare the three different brands on features that are very important to me, like arch support, lacing pattern, and cushioning. Based on what I learned, I felt pretty good about Brand Z, and so I purchased this brand at my favorite sporting goods store."

Hierarchy of Effects likely utilized by Ashley S.: *THE STANDARD LEARNING HIERARCHY*

Part 2

The structure of each Hierarchy of Effects holds important implications regarding the development of marketing strategies.

The Standard Learning Hierarchy

In the Standard Learning Hierarchy, attitudes are largely structured around relatively effortful cognition, or the considered beliefs that a consumer has about products/services. Because of this, marketers must be most concerned with the belief structures that surround their products/services and their competitors' products/services. If this hierarchy is used, then in order to influence that consumer's attitude, a marketer must first and foremost be concerned with managing the beliefs that consumers possess about products/services.

The Low-Involvement Hierarchy

In the Low-Involvement Hierarchy, behavior is not based on either elaborate beliefs or strong emotions, but rather is based on very rudimentary knowledge surrounding the product/service. Because purchase tends to occur in the absence of either elaborate beliefs or strongly felt emotions, the purchase behavior may be influenced by other factors. Behavioral Learning models such as Operant Conditioning and Classical Conditioning often play an important role here. The promise of a reward for behavior might influence purchase decisions. In addition, the creation of perceived associations between positive stimuli and your brand might influence purchase decisions.

The Experiential Hierarchy

In the Experiential Hierarchy, behavior is based on strongly felt emotions. Because purchase/nonpurchase decisions are based on affect, marketers must pay special attention to the emotional, experiential, and aesthetic aspects of their product/service. Therefore, design aspects of the product/service play a very important role here. The design of a product includes its aesthetic dimensions (for example, factors such as style, color, and form) as well as experiential factors such as perceived usability. Design issues have become increasingly important to marketers over the past few decades.

Please answer the following three questions:

1. You are responsible for Brand Y. If you were focused on winning over Terry M. to your brand, what general marketing strategy might you employ?

2. You are responsible for Brand Z. If you were focused on winning over Chris R. to your brand, what general marketing strategy might you employ?

3. You are responsible for Brand X. If you were focused on winning over Ashley S. to your brand, what general marketing strategy might you employ?

20. The Fishbein Model of Attitude Measurement

The Fishbein Model is one model within a group of models known as the Multiattribute Models. These models are used to measure and quantify consumers' attitudes. Specifically, the Fishbein model is used to measure consumers' attitudes toward a number of competing brands by measuring consumers' perceptions of the degree to which each of those brands possesses certain attributes, and the degree to which those attributes are important to the consumer.

The formula for the Fishbein model is:

$$A(o) = \sum_{i=1}^{m} (B_i \times E_i)$$

where:

A(o)	= attitude toward the object/brand
B_i	= belief that object/brand possesses attribute i
E_i	= evaluation of the importance/desirability of attribute i
i	= attribute 1, 2, ...m

The *types* of information that we collect when utilizing the Fishbein multiattribute attitude model are fairly standard. As noted above, the model collects two types of information: consumers' perceptions of the degree to which each brand possesses certain attributes, and the degree to which those attributes are important/desirable to the consumer. However, there are many different *ways* in which to gather this information. Researchers have used Likert scales, rating scales, semantic differential scales, constant sum scales, etc., to gather this data.

The following is an example of how researchers might use specific questions to measure and quantify consumers' attitudes toward three brands of refrigerators. This particular example utilizes a *constant sum scale* and *Likert scales* to obtain the information necessary for the Fishbein model.

Example

We are interested in understanding the importance and desirability of different features of refrigerators. Please divide 100 points among the following features to reflect their relative importance to you when making a purchase decision in the product category of refrigerators:

Price	_____
Energy Efficiency	_____
Brand Reputation	_____
Flexible Shelving	_____
	100 points

Please place an X on each of the following scales to reflect your beliefs regarding how three brands of refrigerators rate on these features:

I believe the Brand A refrigerator is priced reasonably.

Strongly _ _ _ _ _ _ _ Strongly
Disagree   1   2   3   4   5   6   7   Agree

I believe the Brand B refrigerator is priced reasonably.

Strongly _ _ _ _ _ _ _ Strongly
Disagree   1   2   3   4   5   6   7   Agree

I believe the Brand C refrigerator is priced reasonably.

Strongly _ _ _ _ _ _ _ Strongly
Disagree   1   2   3   4   5   6   7   Agree

I believe the Brand A refrigerator is energy efficient.

Strongly _ _ _ _ _ _ _ Strongly
Disagree   1   2   3   4   5   6   7   Agree

I believe the Brand B refrigerator is energy efficient.

Strongly _ _ _ _ _ _ _ Strongly
Disagree   1   2   3   4   5   6   7   Agree

I believe the Brand C refrigerator is energy efficient.

Strongly _ _ _ _ _ _ _ Strongly
Disagree   1   2   3   4   5   6   7   Agree

I believe the Brand A refrigerator has a strong brand reputation.

Strongly _ _ _ _ _ _ _ Strongly
Disagree   1   2   3   4   5   6   7   Agree

I believe the Brand B refrigerator has a strong brand reputation.

Strongly _ _ _ _ _ _ _ Strongly
Disagree   1   2   3   4   5   6   7   Agree

I believe the Brand C refrigerator has a strong brand reputation.

Strongly _ _ _ _ _ _ _ Strongly
Disagree   1   2   3   4   5   6   7   Agree

I believe the Brand A refrigerator has flexible shelving.

Strongly _ _ _ _ _ _ _ Strongly
Disagree   1   2   3   4   5   6   7   Agree

I believe the Brand B refrigerator has flexible shelving.

Strongly _ _ _ _ _ _ _ Strongly
Disagree   1   2   3   4   5   6   7   Agree

I believe the Brand C refrigerator has flexible shelving.

Strongly _ _ _ _ _ _ _ Strongly
Disagree   1   2   3   4   5   6   7   Agree

Please place yourselves in the following situation:

You are the regional account manager for a line of printer/copiers that are specifically targeted toward small business offices that include 10–35 employees. You are interested in increasing sales to real estate offices in your region. You know that the purchase decision regarding printer/copiers is usually made by the office manager in small real estate offices, and you want to gather more information about the attitudes of real estate office managers toward your brand of printer/copier (Brand A), and your two closest competitors' printer/copiers (Brands B and C). You and your two competitors currently offer very similar pricing schedules and service contracts to real estate offices, so price and service are unlikely to be differentiating attributes that would influence office managers' attitudes toward the products.

Part 1

Using a separate document, develop a questionnaire that could be used to measure office managers' attitude scores toward each of the three brands (Brands A, B, and C) of printer/copiers. Please make this questionnaire as realistic as possible, using the example above as your guide when developing respondent instructions and response scales. Use three attributes:
- Print quality
- Speed of printing/copying
- Ease of use

Part 2

After developing the questionnaire, answer the questions yourself (any answers will do—they are all hypothetical).

Part 3

Using the answers that you gave in Part 2, calculate your attitude score toward each brand of printer/copier. *Show all of your work.*

21. The Extended Fishbein Model

(Please note: Complete the previous case, "The Fishbein Model and Attitude Measurement" before beginning this case)

In the previous case, "The Fishbein Model and Attitude Measurement," you developed a questionnaire that could be used to gather information for the Fishbein model to measure real estate office managers' attitudes toward three different brands of printer/copiers—yours (Brand A) and two competitors' (Brands B and C).

Please now place yourselves in the following situation:

The results of this Fishbein study showed that office managers' attitude scores toward Brands B and C were both higher than their attitude scores toward your brand (Brand A). However, something doesn't seem right about this study, since sales of your brand have been outpacing both of the competing brands in this target market.

You know that the Fishbein model has been criticized as too simplistic, and you wonder if there isn't a more comprehensive model that you might use. Specifically, the original Fishbein has been criticized because it measures a customer's attitude toward a brand, rather than toward the purchase of that brand. You know, for instance, that even though you have a great attitude toward all the attributes of Rolls Royce cars, your attitude toward *purchasing* one would be very negative—on your salary, it would put you in the poorhouse!

Another criticism of the original Fishbein is that it makes no attempt to take reference group influences into account. Both of these are valid criticisms, and you decide to create another questionnaire, which would gather the information that would allow you to utilize the Extended Fishbein Model (also sometimes called the Theory of Reasoned Action).

The Extended Fishbein model addresses both of the criticisms of the original Fishbein model by measuring customers' attitudes toward the act of purchase (rather than attitude toward the object/brand), and also attempting to measure customers' perceptions regarding what others in their lives want them to purchase. In this way, the Extended Fishbein model is a better measure of customers' behavioral intent toward the brand (whether the customer intends to buy the brand), rather than their attitude toward the brand.

According to the Extended Fishbein Model, Behavioral Intent (BI) is influenced by two factors:

- Attitude-Toward-the-Action—*A(act):* One's overall appraisal of a behavior/purchase measured by one's beliefs and evaluations of the consequences of that behavior/purchase.

- Subjective Norms—*SN*: One's beliefs regarding significant others' expectations/desires regarding the behavior/purchase and one's motivation to comply with these expectations/desires.

Specifically, the formula for the Extended Fishbein Model is as follows:

$$\textbf{BI} = \textbf{w1 [A(act)]} + \textbf{w2 [SN(act)]}$$

where:

BI	= Behavioral Intent
w1 and w2	= weights (typically these are previously determined)
A(act)	= Attitude toward an action (e.g., purchase)
SN(act)	= Subjective Norm

A(act) is further defined as:

$$A(act) = \sum_{i=1}^{m} (Bi \times Ei)$$

where:

Bi	= Belief that an action (e.g., purchase) will lead to a consequence i
Ei	= Evaluation of importance/desirability of consequence i
i	= consequences 1,2, ...m

SN(act) is further defined as:

$$SN(act) = \sum_{j=1}^{n} (NBj \times MCj)$$

where:

NBj	= Belief that a reference group (j) wants you to perform an action (e.g., purchase)
MCj	= Motivation to comply with reference group j
j	= reference groups 1,2, ...n

Recently, you heard that the company marketing Brand C printer/copiers decided to stop offering the special pricing schedule that they had previously made available to real estate companies. Since this significantly increases the price of the Brand C printer/copiers to real estate offices, there are really only two main competitors left in the region—your brand and Brand B.

You know that you must focus on consequences rather than attributes when utilizing the Extended Fishbein Model, so you change each of the attributes used in the original Fishbein study so that the attribute "print quality" becomes "the ability to create high-quality documents," "speed of printing/copying" becomes "I don't waste time printing or making copies," and "ease of use" becomes "anyone can easily use the printer/copier."

When considering the reference groups that might be important to office managers in this purchase situation, you decide to use two reference groups: the office manager's boss and the realtors in the office.

You also do some background work and find that in similar studies, it has been found that the Attitude-Toward-the-Act component is a slightly more important determinant of Behavioral Intent than is the Subjective Norm component. Therefore, you set **w1 at 0.6 and w2 at 0.4.**

Now that you have developed the Extended Fishbein questionnaire, you want to implement a test of the questionnaire before sending it out to all of your target customers. One of your favorite customers, Betsy, who is the office manager of a real estate office in Lawton, Oklahoma, has agreed to serve as your test subject for this questionnaire. You send the questionnaire to her and wait for her response.

One week later Betsy returns the completed questionnaire. Assume that Betsy has answered the questions in the manner shown below:

Questionnaire (with Betsy's answers)

Please place an X on each of the scales to reflect your level of agreement or disagreement with the following statements:

1. It is important to me that I have the ability to create high-quality documents.
   Strongly __ __ __ __ __ _x_ __ *Strongly*
   Disagree -3 -2 -1 0 1 2 3 *Agree*

2. I believe that if I buy Brand A I will have the ability to create high-quality documents.
   Strongly _x_ __ __ __ __ __ __ *Strongly*
   Disagree -3 -2 -1 0 1 2 3 *Agree*

3. I believe that if I buy Brand B I will have the ability to create high-quality documents.
   Strongly __ __ __ __ __ _x_ __ *Strongly*
   Disagree -3 -2 -1 0 1 2 3 *Agree*

4. It is important to me that I don't waste time printing or making copies.
   Strongly __ __ __ __ __ __ _x_ *Strongly*
   Disagree -3 -2 -1 0 1 2 3 *Agree*

5. I believe that if I buy Brand A I will not waste time printing or making copies.
   Strongly __ __ __ __ __ _x_ __ *Strongly*
   Disagree -3 -2 -1 0 1 2 3 *Agree*

6. I believe that if I buy Brand B I will not waste time printing or making copies.
   Strongly __ _x_ __ __ __ __ __ *Strongly*
   Disagree -3 -2 -1 0 1 2 3 *Agree*

7. It is important to me that anyone can easily use the printer/copier.
   Strongly _x_ __ __ __ __ __ __ *Strongly*
   Disagree -3 -2 -1 0 1 2 3 *Agree*

8. I believe that if I buy Brand A anyone will be able to easily use the printer/copier.
   Strongly _x_ __ __ __ __ __ __ *Strongly*
   Disagree -3 -2 -1 0 1 2 3 *Agree*

9. I believe that if I buy Brand B anyone will be able to easily use the printer/copier.

Strongly   __ __ __ __ __ __x__   *Strongly*
Disagree   -3 -2 -1 0 1 2 3   *Agree*

10. It is important to me to go along with what my boss wants me to do.

Strongly   __ __ __ __ __x__ __   *Strongly*
Disagree   -3 -2 -1 0 1 2 3   *Agree*

11. I believe that my boss wants me to buy Brand A.

Strongly   __ __ __ __ __ __x__   *Strongly*
Disagree   -3 -2 -1 0 1 2 3   *Agree*

12. I believe that my boss wants me to buy Brand B.

Strongly   __ __ __ __x__ __ __   *Strongly*
Disagree   -3 -2 -1 0 1 2 3   *Agree*

13. It is important to me to go along with what the realtors in the office want me to do.

Strongly   __ __x__ __ __ __   *Strongly*
Disagree   -3 -2 -1 0 1 2 3   *Agree*

14. I believe that the realtors in the office want me to buy Brand A.

Strongly   __ __ __ __x__ __ __   *Strongly*
Disagree   -3 -2 -1 0 1 2 3   *Agree*

15. I believe that the realtors in the office want me to buy Brand B.

Strongly   __ __ __ __ __ __x__   *Strongly*
Disagree   -3 -2 -1 0 1 2 3   *Agree*

Please do the following:

1. Use the Extended Fishbein formula, the previous information regarding w1 and w2, and Betsy's questionnaire answers to calculate her Behavioral Intent toward *each* of the two competing brands of printer/copiers (Brand A and Brand B). *Show all of your work/calculations.*

   (Hint: You may want to begin by identifying the type of information that each of the items on the questionnaire is designed to gather: B, E, NB, or MC).

2. Discuss the implications of your results and of Betsy's answers. What have you learned? Were there any surprises in Betsy's answers?

SECTION VIII:

MARKETING COMMUNICATIONS AND ATTITUDE CHANGE

22. Multiattribute Models and Attitude Change Strategies

Fivestar, Inc., is a regional tire manufacturer with sales in the Northeastern United States. They have been in business for over two decades, but remain disappointed with their market share in the winter (snow) tire category. The original product introduction of Treadfast, their winter tire, stressed the price differential between the Treadfast tires and the more widely recognized national brands. Initial sales were encouraging, but sales quickly leveled off, and Treadfast's share of the Northeastern winter tire market has proven to be lower than expected. Fivestar's advertising campaign for the Treadfast tires continues to emphasize the price of the tires, with the tagline "All the traction of the better-known tires, at a price you can afford."

The marketing manager at Fivestar recently retired, and a new marketing manager, Craig Harris, was brought on board. In assessing the products that he would be responsible for, Craig was especially critical of the Treadfast winter tire. He felt that the product had significant potential in the marketplace, but that for some reason this potential had not yet been realized. During his first few months on the job, he made a proposal to senior management requesting that funds be provided to conduct a market research study in this area. The request was approved, and Craig hired a market research firm, Kelsey and Mackenzie Inc. (known as K&M) to conduct the study.

In the exploratory phase of the research, K&M conducted three focus groups in three different cities in the Northeast region of the United States. The primary objective of these three focus groups was to identify the evaluative criteria that consumers use when making a winter tire purchase decision. Four criteria were consistently mentioned throughout each of the focus groups: (1) traction/tread, (2) puncture resistance, (3) price, and (4) warranty/expected life of the tire.

The next phase of the research involved surveying recent winter tire purchasers to establish (1) the relative importance of each of these four evaluative criteria, and (2) consumers' perceptions of Treadfast's and three major competitors' performance on each of the four evaluative criteria (on a scale of 1–10, with 10 being the most positive). The results of this survey were surprisingly similar throughout the different segments of the winter tire market. A table depicting the typical results of this survey follows:

| Attribute | Attribute Importance | "Treadfast" | Brand Scores | | |
			"Bridgeyear"	"Goodstone"	"Linemich"
Traction	35	4	8	7	9
Puncture Res.	30	3	3	3	3
Affordability	15	8	4	6	2
Warranty	20	7	5	4	5

As part of the open-ended questions section at the end of the survey, researchers noted that many respondents cited noise levels as a reason for dissatisfaction with their purchase. In other words, whereas the loudness of the tire had not been an important criterion that they considered when making their purchase decision, it became a significant issue after the purchase when the noise levels were considerably higher than anticipated. Researchers further noted that while these complaints showed up with some frequency among those purchasers of all three competitors' tires, they were virtually nonexistent among the purchasers of the Treadfast tires.

When researchers at K&M presented their findings to senior management at Fivestar, it was obvious to everyone present that the attempted positioning of the Treadfast winter tire, "All the traction of the better-known tires, at a price you can afford," had been largely unsuccessful. Whereas consumers perceived the Treadfast tire as affordable, they did not think that it offered "all the traction of the better-known tires." Fivestar managers were understandably upset by the research findings, and expressed these feelings to Laura Frederick, the K&M account manager responsible for the Treadfast research project.

Laura Frederick had been in the marketing research field for many years, and was experienced at delivering research results to clients in situations where the results were sure to be viewed as bad news. She knew that the presentation required her to be tactful, sensitive to their disappointment, and persuasive in convincing them to focus on future opportunities rather than past failures.

After a lengthy discussion of the research findings, Laura said, "We've spent a lot of time so far analyzing consumers' attitudes toward the Treadfast tire and its three major competitors. This time and effort has been well spent, because we are now in the very fortunate position of having a comprehensive understanding of consumers' attitudes."

Laura went on to say that although the results of the research didn't represent good news, this comprehensive understanding of current consumer attitudes was crucial to future discussions regarding the ways in which Fivestar might be able to successfully *change* consumers' attitudes. For example, if attitudes are defined as a combination of consumers' beliefs about the degree to which brands possess certain attributes, together with their feelings regarding the importance of those attributes, then strategies regarding how to successfully change those attitudes typically fall into three basic approaches:

1. *Changing the importance/desirability of attribute(s):* This usually entails emphasizing the importance of an attribute on which your brand rates particularly well, de-emphasizing an attribute on which your brand rates particularly low, or both.

2. *Changing brand belief(s):* For example, one might choose to use advertising to show consumers that your brand is more positive on a certain attribute, and/or a competing brand is more negative on that attribute, than they had previously believed.

3. *Adding a new attribute(s):* This might include making consumers aware of an attribute that they hadn't previously considered when making a purchase decision, and/or adding a feature to your brand that the competing brands don't possess.

Please do the following:

Using the three broad approaches to attitude change listed previously, come up with *specific* examples of how *each* of these three different approaches might be used to change consumers' attitudes toward the Treadfast tire. In order to do this, you should rely heavily on the consumer attitude survey results revealed by K&M. Please note that your task is to identify the different specific strategies that might be used to change consumers' attitudes toward the Treadfast tire, *not* the specific ads that might be used to carry out these strategies.

1. Describe one strategy through which Fivestar might be able to change consumers' attitudes toward Treadfast by **changing the importance/desirability of attribute(s)**.

2. Describe one strategy through which Fivestar might be able to change consumers' attitudes toward Treadfast by **changing brand belief(s)**.

3. Describe one strategy through which Fivestar might be able to change consumers' attitudes toward Treadfast by **adding a new attribute(s)**.

23. The Elaboration Likelihood Model

The Elaboration Likelihood Model (ELM) highlights two different marketing communication strategies that can be used to create attitude change in consumers. Decisions regarding which of these two strategies should be utilized are based on the probable involvement level of the intended audience. If the intended audience is likely to be highly involved in a product category, marketers should use the "Central Route" to persuasion. If, on the other hand, the intended audience is not likely to be involved in a product category, marketers should use the "Peripheral Route" to persuasion.

According to the Elaboration Likelihood Model, consumers under high involvement conditions diligently process message information and form "cognitive responses" to persuasive communications. Attitude change through this route is typically accomplished by providing receivers with information-rich messages that change their belief structures. Attitude change via this Central Route is often strong and enduring.

In contrast, consumers under low involvement conditions act as cognitive misers, and may respond on a largely unconscious level to peripheral cues in the marketing communication (e.g., humor, beautiful images, etc.). This route is sometimes viewed as a form of classical conditioning, since attitude change through this route is typically accomplished by associating one's brand with other positive stimuli. This route may also make use of the "mere exposure" effect, whereby consumers like a brand more if they are more familiar with it. Attitude change via this Peripheral Route is often much weaker than the type of attitude change that results from the Central Route.

As noted above, if audience members are highly involved in a product category, they are likely to make the effort to process the information in a marketing communication message. Therefore, the marketer should take this important opportunity to convey strong and detailed reasons why the consumer should choose their brand. If the marketer instead chooses to merely convey "feel good" messages concerning their brand, they have wasted a valuable opportunity to create true and lasting attitude change in the audience members.

On the other hand, if audience members are not involved in a product category, they are not likely to be motivated to process the information in a marketing communication. In this case, audience members would be overwhelmed by an information-rich message, would suffer from "Information Overload," and would process very little of the information in the message. Therefore, an information-rich marketing communication strategy directed toward low involvement consumers would be a waste of resources and unlikely to achieve any attitude change. Given a low involvement audience, it is far more effective to focus on achieving incremental increases in consumers' positive feelings toward a brand. Although attitude change achieved through this Peripheral Route is likely to be much weaker than attitude change achieved through the Central Route, it still constitutes attitude change. And since the Central Route is not available to you with these low involvement consumers, the Peripheral Route to attitude change is the only option available.

Please place yourselves in the following situation:

You work for a camping and hiking gear manufacturer, WildernessGear. Your R&D people have just developed an incredible new material that resists water better than any material on the market, is more durable, and lighter in weight. You are very excited about communicating the specifics of this new material to your customers, and are meeting with your advertising agency people this afternoon to discuss the marketing communications campaign you plan to implement. Your chief marketing officer (CMO) has just stopped by your office to see how your preparations for the meeting are going.

You: This new campaign is going to be great. I've got all the data from the R&D people—here, take a look at it. The rain resistance of this new tent material is 15% better than the best that is on the market today. And—look at this part—the tents will be much less likely to rip, and this new material is even lighter to carry! The marketing communications argument that we can make for buying a tent made of this new material is incredibly strong. I think our customers will really respond to it.

CMO: I think you're right. Our customers will definitely see the value in this new development. I'm pleased that you have ideas about how to convey this data to them in a convincing way. But I wonder if we should be focusing so exclusively on the hikers and camping enthusiasts who will respond to these arguments.

You: What do you mean? That's our market!

CMO: Recently, I've been reading a lot about trends in this industry, and some of the information I've seen points to an increase in interest among consumers who have never hiked or camped before. Apparently, given the difficult economy we are currently faced with, there is growing interest in vacationing close to home, and in a way that is relatively inexpensive. This has spurred a great deal of interest in camping among those who have never camped and don't know anything about camping gear.

You: I've seen some of that information too—that's great news for WildernessGear. Well, we were thinking of placing our new print ads in the magazines that we always use—the ones that cater to hikers and campers. But maybe we should also place them in general interest magazines and pick up some of those potential new customers.

CMO: Yes…but use the same ad in both types of magazines?

You: Sure. As you said, we can make a strong and convincing argument that our new material is technically far superior to our competitors' products.

CMO: Well, I've got another meeting to run to. Let's talk about this later.

The worried look on your CMO's face as she left your office concerns you. Maybe you need to think a little more about this new campaign strategy before the meeting this afternoon. You sit down to sketch out ideas for ads, wondering whether the ads in the two types of magazines, general interest versus camping-related, should indeed be one and the same.

Please do the following:

1. Sketch out the ad that will be run in magazines that cater to hikers and campers, and will therefore reach an audience that is likely to be highly involved in the camping gear product category. This ad should be a one-page print ad and need only be a rough draft (stick figures, etc., work fine here).

2. Sketch out the ad that will be run in general interest magazines, and will therefore reach an audience that is unlikely to be highly involved in the camping gear product category. This ad should be a one-page print ad and need only be a rough draft (stick figures, etc., work fine here).

3. Utilizing concepts inherent to the Elaboration Likelihood Model, discuss how the *content* and *strategies* of these two ads differ.

24. Social Judgment Theory and Attitude Change

Social Judgment Theory involves consumers' existing attitudes and opinions, and how consumers incorporate new information into those preexisting attitudes. In theory, consumers compare an incoming new message about an issue with their existing attitude about that particular issue, and this comparison determines their response to the message. For example, if a consumer held an opinion on an issue that was fairly middle-of-the-road, with a slight tendency to be more negative on the issue than positive, their opinion might be characterized by the X on the scale below (e.g., slightly to the left of center). Surrounding that opinion point is a "latitude of acceptance" (in the lightly shaded area), and beyond that latitude of acceptance are "latitudes of rejection" (in the darkly shaded areas).

	latitude of rejection	latitude of acceptance	latitude of rejection	
(negative)		X		(positive)

According to Social Judgment Theory, if new information related to that issue is received by this consumer and the new information is perceived by this consumer as being somewhat similar to his/her preexisting opinion on the issue, that information will fall within the latitude of acceptance, and the consumer will accept the new information. If new information related to the issue is received by this consumer and is perceived as not being similar to his/her preexisting opinion on the issue, that information will fall within the latitude of rejection, and the consumer will reject the new information.

If the new information falls within the latitude of acceptance, it is likely that an *assimilation effect* will occur. An assimilation effect occurs when incoming information ("O" on the scale below) is perceived as being even more consistent with the preexisting opinion than it actually is. The consumer in effect absorbs the new information into their preexisting opinion. When this happens, the consumer will shift their old, preexisting opinion in the direction of the incoming message.

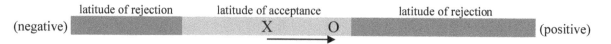

	latitude of rejection	latitude of acceptance	latitude of rejection	
(negative)		X O		(positive)

Attitude shifts in the direction of the incoming information, in this case becoming more positive

If an assimilation effect has occurred, the result is attitude change. The consumer's attitude has shifted in the direction of the incoming message. ("C" on the scale below represents the consumer's changed attitude).

	latitude of rejection	latitude of acceptance	latitude of rejection	
(negative)		C		(positive)

On the other hand, if the new information falls within a latitude of rejection, it is likely that a *contrast effect* will occur. A contrast effect occurs when incoming information ("O" on the scale below) is perceived as being even more dissimilar to the preexisting opinion than it is. The consumer in effect draws a sharp distinction between the incoming message and their own views on the issue. When this happens, the consumer will shift their opinion away from the incoming message.

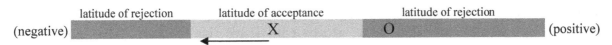

Attitude shifts away from the incoming information, in this case becoming more negative

If a contrast effect has occurred, the result is attitude change. The consumer's attitude has shifted away from the opinion expressed in the incoming message. ("C" on the scale below represents the consumer's changed attitude).

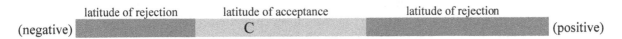

In both cases above, the incoming message expressed a positive view on the issue, attempting to influence the consumer to have a more positive attitude. In the first instance, where the incoming information fell within the consumer's latitude of acceptance, the consumer's attitude became more positive, meaning that this influence attempt was successful. In the second instance, where the information fell within a latitude of rejection, the influence attempt backfired; the consumer's attitude became even more negative.

In constructing marketing messages that are designed to effect attitude change in consumers, it is important to assess not only the preexisting attitudes among message recipients, but also the likely widths of the latitudes of acceptance and rejection. Notably, the more strongly held a preexisting attitude, the *narrower* the latitude of acceptance will be. In other words, if a consumer holds an opinion with great conviction, the width of the latitude of acceptance will be quite small, and the latitudes of rejection quite wide. On the other hand, if the opinion is not a closely held one, the width of the latitude of acceptance will be fairly broad.

Please place yourselves in the following situation:

You work for Stanton, Inc., a company that is one of the largest producers and marketers of distilled spirits in Europe, and the largest wine producing company by volume in the world. You are a category manager for red wines, and your CEO is questioning you about the ways in which sales of red wines to the United States might be increased. He sees opportunity for improvement in sales of red wine to the United States, since these sales numbers per capita have historically lagged behind the per capita sales figures in Europe. He has asked you to investigate the possibility of instituting a marketing communications campaign that would increase primary demand for red wine in the United States, with the knowledge that since Stanton is the world leader in wine production, it stands to gain the most from a successful campaign to increase primary demand in that product category. The CEO feels strongly that this new marketing communications campaign should center around the newly discovered, and much talked about, potential health benefits related to a moderate intake of red wine. Scientists and medical professionals have recently begun to declare that some of the ingredients that are found in red wine may, when taken in moderation, have a positive impact on overall health.

As part of your investigation, you have been researching American consumers' attitudes toward alcohol in general as well as their attitudes toward the potential health benefits of red wine. You have found a very different picture emerging from this investigation than would be found among European consumers. Because of their relatively puritanical history, you have found that many Americans view all alcohol, including wine, as decidedly destructive to health. This is quite different from the attitudes that are typically found among European consumers, who have historically viewed wine as a positive and healthful part of life.

Looking at your research results in more depth, you see that American consumers' attitudes toward the potential health benefits of red wine differ markedly by age group. Older Americans tend to view all alcohol, including red wine, as destructive to health, and they hold this attitude with strong conviction. Younger Americans are slightly more negative than positive about the potential health impact of red wine, but they are much more positive than their older counterparts, and their attitudes are much less rigidly held.

Please do the following:

1. You are developing a presentation to your colleagues at Stanton that will summarize your research findings related to American consumers and the health impact of red wine. You decide to use Social Judgment Theory to help convey the difference in attitude structures between younger and older Americans. Please use the space below to draw the two scales that you would use to depict the attitudes of younger Americans and older Americans on this subject.

2. Once you feel that you have effectively captured the differing attitudes of younger and older Americans toward the health impact of red wine in scale images, it is time to begin brainstorming how your marketing communications appeals to the two groups will differ. Please briefly describe the type of appeal that you will use with older Americans, and also the type of appeal that you will use with younger Americans.

25. Balance Theory and Spokesperson Strategies

Fritz Heider's Balance Theory[1] is part of a group of theories that are based on the *consistency principle*, which basically asserts that human beings are motivated to maintain consistency. Balance Theory specifically addresses consistency among three entities. In marketing applications of this theory, these three entities are typically a person, another person, and an attitude object. The perceived relationships among these three can be either positive or negative. In the image below, the person is identified by C, the other person is identified by S, and the object is identified by O. The three entities and the relationships between them make up an attitude structure called a triad.

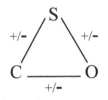

According to Balance Theory, there are two types of relationships that might exist between each of the entities in the triad: a sentiment relation, or a unit relation. A sentiment relation exists when one entity has liking or disliking for another entity, and a unit relation exists when the perception exists that two entities belong together or are connected in some way.

Part 1 *(please finish each part of this case before moving on to the next part of the case)*

As an example, let's say Charlie hates cigarettes and anything having to do with smoking, creating a negative sentiment relation between Charlie (C) and cigarettes (O). Charlie loves his best friend Sam, so obviously Charlie (C) feels a strong positive sentiment for Sam (S). Sam has just taken up smoking, creating a unit relationship between Sam (S) and cigarettes (O). The triad would be depicted as follows:

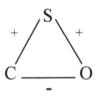

Please answer the following questions:

    1. In your opinion, would this triad feel comfortable to Charlie?

    2. Would Charlie be motivated to resolve this discomfort in some way? What might he do?

---

[1] Heider, F. (1958). *The Psychology of Interpersonal Relations*. New York: John Wiley.

Part 2 *(please finish each part of this case before moving on to the next part of the case)*

From the point of view of the person (symbolized by the C below), are the following triads balanced or unbalanced? *Please write either "balanced" or "unbalanced" under each of the triads depicted below.*

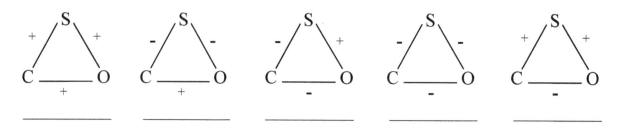

_____ _____ _____ _____ _____

Part 3 *(please finish each part of this case before moving on to the next part of the case)*

In November 2008, General Motors (US) ended a nine-year relationship with Tiger Woods. Tiger was perhaps most visible as a spokesperson for GM's Buick brand, where he served to give the brand a more youthful image. The average age of Buick owners was hovering in the low 70s in 2001, but had dropped to 66 for Buick sedans and 53 for the Buick Enclave by 2008. By all accounts, the Buick/Tiger Woods relationship was a positive one for Tiger Woods as well, with the endorsement deal garnering him at least US$7 million a year.[2]

Whereas the specific reasoning behind the Buick/Tiger Woods marketing campaign is likely known only to GM and the Integrated Marketing Communications professionals who work with that company, one might view that campaign through the lens of Balance Theory as follows.

- A target segment of young consumers (C) perceive the Buick brand as being a brand for elderly people, and they therefore have a negative sentiment toward Buick (O):

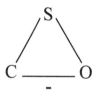

- Tiger Woods (S) is an international sports figure who is well-liked by most consumers in that target segment (C).

[2] Krisher, T. (2008, November 24). "GM Ends 9-Year Tiger Woods Endorsement Deal," *Time*.

- Buick chooses Tiger Woods as a spokesperson for their brand. This, in theory, creates the following unbalanced triad:

According to Balance Theory, an unbalanced triad creates motivation within the person, in this case the target segment consumer (C), to resolve the imbalance. Theoretically, there are three ways that the target consumer (C) might resolve this imbalance:

1. The consumer may decrease positive feelings toward the spokesperson (e.g., the target consumer may decide that they don't like Tiger Woods after all).

2. The consumer may break the connection between the spokesperson and the object (e.g., the target consumer may decide that Tiger Woods doesn't really like the Buick brand; he is only saying so in order to make US$7 million per year).

3. The consumer may increase positive feelings toward the object (e.g., the consumer may decide that Buick must be a good brand if Tiger Woods is its spokesperson).

Obviously, of the three possible resolutions above, marketers who enter into a costly endorsement strategy hope that the third method of resolving the inconsistency in an unbalanced triad is the one that is chosen by consumers. In order to increase the chances that this will be the case, marketers make every attempt to ensure that neither of the first two means of resolution is chosen by consumers. In an attempt to ensure that the first type of resolution (the consumer decreasing positive feelings toward the spokesperson) is not chosen, marketers should select a very well-liked spokesperson. In an attempt to ensure that the second type of resolution (the consumer breaking the connection between the spokesperson and the object) is not chosen, marketers should choose an endorsement strategy that consistently and frequently emphasizes a strong link between the spokesperson and the brand.

Please place yourselves in the following situation:

You work for a lawn mower manufacturer, Don Jeere, Inc., and you are responsible for a new line of simple walk-behind power lawn mowers. In a recent SWOT analysis, executives at Don Jeere identified an increase in purchases of this type of lawn mower by 30-something women. Don Jeere executives interpreted this increase as being the result of two clear cultural trends: more single-parent households headed by a female who performs all house and lawn maintenance herself; and the blurring of strict gender roles in our society. As a consequence of the SWOT analysis, Don Jeere executives have decided to target 30-something women with this Don Jeere walk-behind lawn mower. You are aware that this target segment will be hard to win, since early qualitative research in this area has uncovered an unmistakable tendency for women in this demographic to view the Don Jeere brand of lawn mowers as too expensive for their needs. Nevertheless, the decision has been made to target this demographic with the Don Jeere walk-behind lawn mower line. Don Jeere executives have come up with a comprehensive marketing strategy that includes the use of a spokesperson, but they have not yet chosen who this spokesperson will be. Your task is to identify a spokesperson that you feel would be effective in this situation.

Spokesperson: _____

Part 4 *(please finish each part of this case before moving on to the next part of the case)*

Now that you have identified a potential spokesperson, you should conduct an honest assessment of that spokesperson's "source characteristics." It is probable, given the emphasis on Balance Theory in this exercise, that you have chosen a spokesperson that is very well-liked by members of your target market. This is quite appropriate, given the emphasis on likability in Balance Theory. However, there are many different ways to understand the effectiveness of utilizing spokespeople, and there are many different spokesperson (source) characteristics that may influence the overall effectiveness of a spokesperson in a specific endorsement situation.

Important source characteristics that are often cited include source credibility and source attractiveness. Each of these characteristics can be further broken out into more specific characteristics, such that credibility is broken out into expertise and trustworthiness, and attractiveness is broken out into physical attractiveness, likability, and perceived similarity. So the five source characteristics we will analyze are:

1. Expertise—the degree to which the source of the message is perceived as possessing relevant knowledge, skills, and/or experience.

2. Trustworthiness—the degree to which the source of the message is perceived to be motivated to convey his/her opinions and knowledge honestly.

3. Physical Attractiveness—the degree to which the source of the message is perceived to be good-looking.

4. Likability—the degree to which the source of the message is perceived to be appealing and/or admirable on an interpersonal level.

5. Similarity—the degree to which the source of the message is perceived to be similar to the receiver of the message.

Using the spokesperson that you chose in Part 3, please evaluate that spokesperson on each of these five characteristics by placing a mark on the following 0–10 scales, where 0 indicates that the source characteristic is not at all descriptive of your chosen spokesperson, and 10 indicates that the source characteristic is extremely descriptive of your chosen spokesperson.

Please note that you are not being asked to defend your choice here; please DO NOT merely support your choice by arguing that this particular spokesperson is strong in all important source characteristics. An honest assessment of the spokesperson that you have identified in Part 3 is required here, and is in the best interests of your marketing strategy. In most cases, spokespeople do not possess in strong quantities all of the five source characteristics identified here.

Expertise

| 0 | 1 | 2 | 3 | 4 | 5 | 6 | 7 | 8 | 9 | 10 |

Not at all descriptive   Extremely descriptive

Trustworthiness

| 0 | 1 | 2 | 3 | 4 | 5 | 6 | 7 | 8 | 9 | 10 |

Not at all descriptive   Extremely descriptive

Physical Attractiveness

| 0 | 1 | 2 | 3 | 4 | 5 | 6 | 7 | 8 | 9 | 10 |

Not at all descriptive   Extremely descriptive

Likability

| 0 | 1 | 2 | 3 | 4 | 5 | 6 | 7 | 8 | 9 | 10 |

Not at all descriptive   Extremely descriptive

Similarity

| 0 | 1 | 2 | 3 | 4 | 5 | 6 | 7 | 8 | 9 | 10 |

Not at all descriptive   Extremely descriptive

Part 5 *(please finish each part of this case before moving on to the next part of the case)*

These five Source Characteristics have been the subject of much debate. A 2002 *Journal of Advertising* article notes that one can easily find examples in the marketing literature of researchers who maintain that one or the other of these five source characteristics is, without a doubt, *the* most important source characteristic.[3] In reality, it is likely that different marketing communications situations call for different strengths on the part of the spokesperson.

In general, it is thought that it is most important to use a highly credible source (possessing perceived knowledge and trustworthiness) when the intended receivers of the message view the advertised product as possessing some risk (financial, social, performance, or otherwise). So for a relatively high involvement product, a spokesperson that is perceived as expert and trustworthy may be warranted. In other situations, source credibility may be less important than other source characteristics.

With regard to physical attractiveness, the "match-up hypothesis" postulates that physically attractive spokespeople are more effective endorsers for products that are used to enhance one's attractiveness (e.g., perfume) but may not be as effective as less attractive spokespeople when endorsing products not used to enhance one's own attractiveness (e.g., coffee).

The importance of perceived similarity may also vary with the type of marketing situation. It is generally thought that perceptions of source similarity to self can be especially effective when the intended target consumers feel that the advertised product is "not for them" for one reason or another. Then, if they perceive the spokesperson as having needs, wants, limitations, and life situations similar to their own, they are more likely to accept the implied message that the advertised product will fit those needs, wants, limitations, and/or life situations. For this reason, many marketers choose to use a "typical man/woman on the street" to endorse their product.

Do you wish to change your choice of spokesperson in Part 3? Please answer yes or no and explain why in the space below.

---

[3] Stafford, M. R., Stafford, T. F., & Day, E. (2002). "A Contingency Approach: The Effects of Spokesperson Type and Service Type on Service Advertising Perceptions," *Journal of Advertising*, 18–34.

SECTION IX:

CUSTOMER DECISION MAKING

26. Group/Family Decision Making

When studying group and family decision making, consumer behaviorists are often interested in the different roles that group members play in the consumption process. These roles typically fall into the following eight categories:

- Influencer—influences the purchase decision
- Gatekeeper—controls/influences the flow of information regarding a purchase
- Decider—makes the final decision regarding a purchase
- Buyer—engages in the actual transaction/purchase
- Preparer—prepares the purchased good(s) for use
- User—uses the purchased good(s)
- Maintainer—maintains or takes care of the good(s)
- Disposer—chooses when and/or how to dispose of the good(s)

Scenario

Meg is a skateboarding whiz. She spends almost all of her free time in the driveway of her suburban home, perfecting her skateboarding moves. Recently she saw a "Quarterpipe" ramp in a neighbor's driveway, and she began asking her parents to "please, please" get her one. However, neither Meg nor her parents, Mike and Kathy, knew much about them. One day, Meg's brother Brad sent her some information he pulled off the Internet: step-by-step instructions on how to build a Quarterpipe! He also offered to help her build it when he came home from university in May.

Meg took the information to her parents and begged them to let her build the ramp with Brad. Since Kathy was the one who worried most about Meg's safety when skateboarding, Mike knew he had better leave the decision up to her. After a lot of cajoling, Kathy relented and said alright. She still worried about the safety of the ramp, but she really liked the idea of Meg and Brad working together to build it—she hadn't seen much brother/sister bonding since Brad went off to university.

In late April, Mike took the Quarterpipe instructions that Brad had sent to Meg and used the materials list to buy all the necessary supplies at the local hardware store. A few weeks later, Brad came home for the summer and he and Meg spent five days building the Quarterpipe ramp. It was a big ramp—nearly four feet high and four feet wide and very heavy. They placed some old skateboard wheels on one side so that it could be rolled around, but even with these it was still too heavy for Meg to move. Kathy was concerned that it not sit in the driveway all the time, so her dad, Mike, promised to take care of it by being the one to roll it behind the garage when it wasn't in use.

Meg loved the Quarterpipe and used it every chance she got. Kathy was happy that Meg was so pleased with her new ramp, but still worried about Meg's safety. Kathy continuously reminded Meg that if she ever saw her using the ramp without wearing all her pads and helmet, Kathy would personally be the one to roll the ramp out to the end of the driveway for the trash collectors to pick up.

Please do the following:

Using the previous scenario and background information, identify the character(s) in the scenario who are playing each of the following roles (if you feel that more than one character matches a given role, please list both or all):

Influencer   _____

Gatekeeper   _____

Decider   _____

Buyer   _____

Preparer   _____

User   _____

Maintainer   _____

Disposer   _____

27. Decision Heuristics

Part 1

Please place yourselves in this situation:

You recently purchased your first house, and you love everything about it except for the living room carpeting, which is a horrible shade of purple. You bought the house with plans to replace the carpeting in a neutral beige color. A week after you moved in, a neighbor came over to welcome you to the neighborhood, and you shared your plans for the house. He said, "Oh, we have a carpet store here in town that runs a big sale a few times a year when they discount carpet pretty heavily. Watch for the Apex ad."

Sure enough, about a month later, you see an ad in the Monday morning newspaper:

APEX CARPETS

Brand A Carpet

Valued at $6.00/sq. ft.
NOW $2.00/sq. ft.

Brand B Carpet

Valued at $4.00/sq. ft.
NOW $1.00/sq. ft.

Both of the options in the ad are available in the shade of beige that you are looking for. You decide to purchase. Unfortunately, you are flying out of town that morning, and the sale lasts only that day. You just heard the taxi to the airport honk its horn out front. With no more information than appears in the ad, you must choose one of the two options, stall the taxi driver for a few moments while you verify the measurements of the living room, and phone in your order.

Before turning the page, choose one of the options (Brand A or Brand B) from the ad above.

Your choice: _____

Now that you have chosen Brand A or Brand B (you *have*, haven't you?), please use the space below to describe the evaluation process you utilized to arrive at your decision:

Part 2

Decision Heuristics

A decision heuristic is a shortcut decision rule that a consumer employs, either consciously or unconsciously, to simplify the decision process. Most of us make so many decisions every day that we would be paralyzed if we had to go through a comprehensive, logical decision making process for each of those decisions. Decision making shortcuts, or heuristics, make our lives easier.

A heuristic can be specific (as in the product category-specific assumption that "larger cars are safer") or they can be very general. General heuristics, sometimes also called market-based heuristics, span numerous product categories and have an overarching influence on many of our consumption decisions. For example, some of you may live by the adage, "You get what you pay for." In this case, you are likely to have chosen the $2.00/sq. ft. carpet, since you believe that in most cases, it is wise to pay the higher price and get a better product. The conscious or unconscious assumption that "You get what you pay for" is a heuristic that informs many of your consumption decisions.

On the other hand, some of you may make the conscious or unconscious assumption that "All brands are essentially the same." In this case, you are likely to have chosen the $1.00/sq. ft. carpet, because you believe that since brands are typically very similar, it doesn't make sense to pay more for essentially the same product. The conscious or unconscious assumption that "All brands are essentially the same" is a heuristic that informs many of your consumption decisions.

Still others of you may not ascribe to either of these two common market-based heuristics, and you may not have used a decision heuristic at all; you may have made every attempt to analyze the highest value option while you were making the very quick decision imposed on you in the previous page.

Do you believe that you employed a decision-making heuristic in choosing Brand A versus Brand B above?

Part 3

Intellectual Alibis

The difficulty for consumer researchers arises when attempting to establish how a consumer decision was made. In many cases, consumers are not completely honest with researchers (or friends, or even themselves!) when describing the way in which they arrived at a decision. A perfect example of this is illustrated below through a self-report of a decision-making process shared by a very self-effacing and self-knowledgeable consumer, Scott.

> Very simply, I bought the car because I fell in love with its looks. However, when I told people why I bought the car, I quoted the car's safety ratings and awards. I said it so many times that I think I even began to believe that those were the reasons that I bought the car. But then I remembered that I didn't even know about the safety ratings and awards until *after* I'd already purchased the car, and I was reading all the brochures while the car was sitting in my driveway!

What Scott describes above is a very common phenomenon that marketers call "creating an Intellectual Alibi." Consumers purchase a product based on either a simple heuristic or an emotional response. However, when they are later asked about the purchase, sometimes the simple heuristic or emotional response doesn't "fit" with their vision of how consumers make decisions, so they remember deeper levels of analysis than were actually present during the decision-making process. Some theorists believe that this "revision of history" often happens on an unconscious level; the consumers themselves don't even realize that the reason(s) for purchase they are reporting are not, in actuality, the reasons upon which they based their decisions. Consumers' creation of Intellectual Alibis, whether conscious or unconscious, can make it extremely difficult for consumer researchers to accurately establish the actual reasoning underlying consumers' decision-making processes.

Going back to the carpet example, some of you who utilized a "You get what you pay for" heuristic and who chose Brand A were comfortable giving a simple explanation such as "I always try to buy the more high-end brand; I think it pays off in the long run." However, some of you who also based your decision on the "You get what you pay for" heuristic were not comfortable supplying such a simplistic explanation when you were asked to "describe the evaluation process you utilized to arrive at your decision." In these cases, you likely went back and further analyzed the original ad only *after* you were asked to supply a rationale. In other words, you made a quick choice between Brand A and Brand B (likely based on a decision heuristic), but then when you were asked why you chose that brand, you went back to look at the choices so that you could supply a more analytical answer. Then you likely wrote something like, "I saved $4.00/sq. ft. by buying brand A, whereas I would only have saved $3.00/sq. ft. by buying Brand B."

Correspondingly, some of you who utilized an "All brands are essentially the same" heuristic and who chose Brand B were comfortable giving a simple explanation such as "the two carpets are probably exactly the same, so why would I pay the higher price?" However, some of you who also based your decision on the "All brands are essentially the same" heuristic were not comfortable supplying such a simplistic explanation when you were asked to "describe the evaluation process you utilized to arrive at your decision." In these cases, you likely went back and further analyzed the original ad only *after* you were asked to supply a rationale. In other words, you made a quick choice between Brand A and Brand B (likely based on a decision heuristic), but then when you were asked why you chose that brand, you went back to look at the choices so that you could supply a more analytical answer. Then you likely wrote something like, "I saved 75% by buying brand B, whereas I would only have saved 67% by buying Brand A."

Others of you maintain that you completed a relatively comprehensive, logical analysis prior to making your choice, and then merely described that deliberative process when asked to do so. Only you know the specific decision-making process that you used. Hint: If you found yourself turning the page back to reanalyze the alternatives *after* you had made your decision and were then asked to describe the decision-making process, it is likely that your true decision-making process was the result of a decision heuristic, and your description of the decision-making process was an Intellectual Alibi.

Do you believe that you employed an Intellectual Alibi when asked to "describe the evaluation process you utilized to arrive at your decision?"

Part 4

Decision-Making Approaches and Decision Heuristics

Even for those of you who believe that you completed a relatively comprehensive and logical analysis prior to making your choice, there are some theorists who would argue that the *means* by which you evaluated the decision ($ savings *vs.* % savings) is in itself a reflection of biases related to the particular decision heuristics that you employ.

In other words, those of you who employ the decision heuristic "You get what you pay for" are more likely to have used a comprehensive, analytical decision-making process, which resulted in the choice of the more expensive brand, in this case choosing to save $4.00/sq. ft. by buying Brand A (the more expensive brand), instead of saving $3.00/sq. ft. by buying Brand B. On the other hand, those of you who employ the decision heuristic "All brands are essentially the same" are more likely to have used a comprehensive, analytical decision-making process, which resulted in the choice of the least expensive brand, in this case choosing to save 75% by buying Brand B (the less expensive brand), instead of saving 67% by buying Brand B.

Theorists believe that *even the ways in which you approach a comprehensive, analytical decision-making process* are affected by the unconscious or conscious simplifying decision heuristics that you possess.

Do you believe that the <u>way in which you approached</u> this decision may have been affected by the underlying decision heuristics that you possess?

Part 5

<u>Framing the Message to Overcome Decision Heuristics</u>

A related issue has to do with whether a marketer can frame a message in a way that encourages a specific kind of analytical decision processing rather than a reliance on simplifying decision heuristics.

You be the judge:

For those of you who chose Brand A, would the following ad have led you to a different choice?

Brand A Carpet
67% Off!!!!
Valued at $6.00/sq. ft.
NOW $2.00/sq. ft.

Brand B Carpet
75% OFF!!!!
Valued at $4.00/sq. ft.
NOW $1.00/sq. ft.

For those of you who chose Brand B, would the following ad have led you to a different choice?

Brand A Carpet
Save $4.00/sq. ft.!!!!
Valued at $6.00/sq. ft.
NOW $2.00/sq. ft.

Brand B Carpet
Save $3.00/sq. ft.!!!!
Valued at $4.00/sq. ft.
NOW $1.00/sq. ft.

28. Decision Rules I: Introduction to Decision Rules

It is early in the year 2008, and a major U.S. electronics manufacturer, Trentron, Inc., has been studying the possibility of entering the digital camera market. In the past, it has been a successful strategy for Trentron to play the role of market follower. It has typically watched a new market closely, then chosen to enter once the market is strong for that product; it has had a chance to watch and learn from the experiences, successes, and failures of the early market entrants. Now that digital cameras are a strong market, Trentron is seriously studying the possibility of joining that industry.

Because the digital camera market represents a new consumer market for Trentron, it has been working closely with The ConRes Group, a market research firm specializing in consumer research. The project manager at ConRes who has been responsible for this project has been Tyrone Crandall. When the project was first negotiated between Trentron and ConRes, Tyrone was adamant that the research should be exploratory in nature, and should focus on the ways in which consumers make brand purchase decisions in this market. He felt strongly that this exploratory research should contain two stages.

In the first stage, in-depth interviews would be conducted with qualified consumers to establish the relative importance that they attached to different purchase criteria (or product attributes) and their perceptions regarding the performance of each of the four major brands on each of these purchase criteria (secondary research had already provided Tyrone with the four brands most widely considered by consumers and the five criteria upon which they were likely to rate those brands). For the implementation of this first stage of the research, Tyrone suggested that ConRes place well-trained interviewers outside major electronics stores to qualify consumers (find those consumers who were currently in the market for a digital camera) and then interview the qualified consumers. As an incentive for consumers to agree to participate in the fairly time-consuming interview, ConRes would provide participating consumers with a rebate form that, when sent back to ConRes along with a receipt proving purchase of any digital camera within one month of the interview, would entitle the consumer to receive $25 by mail.

In the second stage of the research, ConRes would contact those interviewed consumers who had sent back the rebate form proving that they had purchased a digital camera, and ask them to take part in a focus group. They would be offered $100 to participate in the focus groups, which would each include around a dozen recent digital camera purchasers as the focus group participants, would last about two hours, and would take place at various times at the ConRes facility. During these focus groups, the recent camera purchasers would discuss many topics having to do with their camera purchase, but special attention would be paid to the process they used to arrive at a purchase decision.

That contract between Trentron and ConRes—detailing the two stages of the proposed exploratory research program—was successfully negotiated in fall 2007. It is now February 2008, and last week Tyrone Crandall received a very attractive employment offer from a competitor of ConRes. He opted to take the offer. Because Tyrone would be working for a competing firm, when he gave notice to ConRes he was immediately escorted from the ConRes property, thereby keeping him from bringing someone else up to date on important projects and seamlessly turning his current projects over to a successor.

Janet Tillman, an analyst with ConRes, has been approached by her boss and asked to take over the Trentron project until a successor to Tyrone can be chosen. Janet has not been affiliated with the ConRes/Trentron project team, but since she is interested in being considered for the project manager position vacated by Tyrone, she jumped at the unique opportunity to prove her abilities to senior management at ConRes. However, now that she has accepted the challenge, she is finding herself somewhat at a loss. Upon obtaining the Trentron project file, it became apparent that although Tyrone may have had many well-thought-out ideas with regard to the culmination of the Trentron case, he was not in the habit of writing these down. Janet found only four documents in the Trentron file: (1) the contract between Trentron and ConRes; (2) the data from the in-depth field interviews conducted as part of stage one of the research; (3) the transcripts of the four focus groups that were conducted in stage two of the research, and (4) a memo Tyrone had written to the executives at Trentron asking them to reconsider a decision to terminate the research after only the first stage of the research had been completed (apparently this memo had been successful, since the results of stage two were sitting right in front of Janet!). The memo has been reproduced here:

****

MEMORANDUM

To: Trentron Executives; Digital Camera NPD Team
From: Tyrone M. Crandall, The ConRes Group
Date: December 16, 2007
Re: Necessity of completing second stage of exploratory research

Let me begin by saying that I fully understand your concern regarding the cost overruns encountered in the first stage of this exploratory research. At times it can be difficult to accurately predict consumer response to our efforts, and that was certainly the case here. Although it is unusual for us to see the very high response rates we encountered in this project (nearly one-third of those qualified consumers who were asked to participate in an in-depth interview by our trained interviewers agreed to do so), and even more unusual to encounter the high number of consumers who took advantage of our rebate incentive (over half of those interviewed sent in the rebate form within one month), I urge you to see both of these surprises as happy circumstances. These numbers provide us with fertile ground for the next, necessary, stage of this research project.

Whereas it may be tempting to conclude that we have obtained, through the interviews, enough information to terminate this research project, I must argue strongly that this is not the case. As you know, the first stage of this project involved the collection of information including consumers' perceptions regarding the importance of various product attributes, and how they saw each of four leading brands performing on those attributes. It is always tempting to believe that once we have collected this detailed information, we can, with confidence, predict the choice that a consumer will make.

Nothing could be further from the truth. The reason for this is that consumers actually use these perceptions about the performance of alternative brands on important attributes in very different ways when making a purchase decision. In fact, it is not uncommon for two consumers who share exactly the same perceptions regarding the major brands and importance of different attributes in a given decision situation to make very different purchase choices due to the different approaches they take to decision making. We refer to these different approaches as Decision Rules. I have taken the liberty of including in this memo descriptions of some Decision Rules that we might expect to see employed in a decision situation involving a digital camera (please see below).

Again, I urge you to reconsider your suggestion to cancel the second stage of this research project. In the first stage of this research project we collected valuable information about the perceptions upon which consumers base their purchase decisions. In the second stage of this project, we will gather information regarding *how* the actual decisions are made.

I look forward to hearing that you've decided to continue with Stage Two of this research project.

Very brief descriptions of some common Decision Rules are included here:

Conjunctive Rule: The consumer sets minimum cutoff scores for each of the evaluative attributes (the cutoffs for each attribute may be set at different levels and are all typically fairly low). Brands that meet ALL of the different attribute cutoff points are kept in consideration.

Lexicographic Rule: The consumer ranks evaluative attributes by importance. He/she looks at the most important attribute and chooses the brand that performs best on that attribute. If two or more brands tie for the highest performance on that attribute, these tying brands are then evaluated with regard to the next most important attribute, and the highest performer is chosen. If two or more brands tie for the highest performance on that attribute, these tying brands are then evaluated with regard to the next most important attribute, and so on down the ranking of attributes, until one brand is left.

Elimination-by-Aspects Rule: The consumer ranks evaluative attributes by importance and sets minimum cutoff points for each attribute (the cutoffs for each attribute may be set at different levels). He/she starts with the most important attribute, and eliminates all those brands that don't meet the minimum cutoff point. The brands remaining are then evaluated on the next most important attribute, and again, those brands that don't meet the cutoff point on this attribute are eliminated from further consideration. This continues until one brand remains.

Compensatory Rules: These rules are characterized by the consumer taking an overall view of each brand. In this way, a brand's poor performance on one attribute may be offset, or compensated for, by high performance on another attribute.

For example, one type of Compensatory Rule is the Weighted Compensatory Rule. In this rule, the consumer assigns a "weight" to each of the product attributes to reflect that attribute's importance to him/her. Then, for each brand, the consumer multiplies the attribute importance weight by that brand's rating on the attribute, thereby obtaining a weighted score on each attribute for that brand. When all of these weighted scores are added together, the consumer has an overall score for that brand. The brand with the highest overall score is chosen.

****

To date, no analyses of the data, either the in-depth interview results or the focus group transcripts, had apparently been undertaken. Janet decided to take a look at the focus group transcripts first. Although this information was the last to be gathered in the chronology of the research project, Janet had always found that one was able to garner the best "feel" for a market by reading the comments of consumers. She read the transcripts of the four focus groups, paying special attention to consumer comments regarding how their purchase decisions were made.

Excerpts of a focus group conducted on January 8, 2008 are reproduced here:

Mark G.:   "Price was my most important feature in choosing a digital camera from the four alternative brands I had identified. I looked at all the digital cameras with this in mind, and got rid of those whose price was higher than I was willing to pay. The next most important feature to me was print quality, so then I got rid of those remaining digital cameras whose print quality was lower than I was looking for. The next most important feature to me was weight, and I rejected those digital cameras that had weights above a certain limit. At this point, only one digital camera remained, and this is the digital camera I bought."

Patricia L.:   "I looked at the feature that was most important to me and planned to choose the digital camera that was best on that feature. When two digital cameras proved to be equally great on that feature, I looked at my next most important feature and that broke the tie."

Kelsey K.:   "I chose the digital camera that was the best when I balanced the good with the bad."

Laura M.:   "I ranked the features that were most important to me, and, starting with the most important feature, got rid of any digital camera that didn't meet my standard with regard to that feature. Then I went to the next most important feature and did the same thing, and so on down the list of features. Eventually only one digital camera was left."

Ron J.:   "I picked the digital camera that had no really bad features."

Bruce F.:   "I looked at all aspects at once. For instance, one digital camera might have had really bad scores on some attributes, but those could be offset by very good scores on other attributes. I wanted the digital camera that was the best overall."

Meghan E.:   "I ranked the features of the digital cameras in terms of importance to me. Then I looked at the feature that was most important to me and chose the digital camera that scored best with regard to that feature."

Doris A.:   "I ended up buying the digital camera that met my minimum standards on all features."

Please do the following:

Read the excerpts from the focus group conducted on January 8, 2008, that are provided as part of this case. Use your understanding of Decision Rules to assess which of the four types of Decision Rules: *Conjunctive, Lexicographic, Elimination-by-Aspects,* or *Compensatory* that each focus group member likely used (Hint: each of the four types of Decision Rules is represented twice).

Mark G.: → COMPENSATORY RULE
          ~~LEXICOGRAPHIC RULE~~

② Patricia L.: LEXICOGRAPHIC RULE

Kelsey K.:- COMPENSATORY RULE

① Laura M.: — ELIMINATION BY ASPECTS

Ron J.: — ELIMINATION BY ASPECTS

③ Bruce F.: — COMPENSATORY RULE

Meghan E.: — LEXICOGRAPHIC RULE

④ Doris A.:- CONJUNCTIVE RULE

29. Decision Rules II: The Application of Decision Rules

(Please note: complete the previous case, "Decision Rules I: Introduction to Decision Rules" before beginning this case.)

Janet is nervous about her upcoming introductory meeting with Trentron executives. Through her discussions with some coworkers who were tangentially involved in the project, she knows that these executives agreed to the second stage of the research project only grudgingly. While Tyrone's memo of December 16 was persuasive, they still didn't quite understand how consumers with exactly the same perceptions could then choose different brands of cameras. One way that she might be able to gain credibility with these clients would be to show them—with their own data—how this can and does happen. Janet searched the data to find consumers whose "tables," those summaries of consumer perceptions generated through the in-depth interviews, matched exactly.

She found four interviewees who each attached the same levels of importance to the five product attributes and rated the brands in exactly the same way in terms of their performance on each of these attributes. The table below represents these four consumers' responses within the in-depth interviews, and specifically identifies: (1) the relative importance of each of the attributes investigated (100 points were distributed among the five attributes to reflect their importance); and (2) the numbers indicating how well they perceived each alternative brand of camera as scoring with respect to each attribute (on a scale of 1 to 10, with 10 representing the most positive score).

Product Attributes	Importance Rating	Brand Scores				CM	EAM
		Brand A	Brand B	Brand C	Brand D		
Print Quality	35	7	3	4	7	4	5
Price	25	5	9	10	8	4	5
Zoom Capability	10	1	9	6	5	4	5
Battery Life	10	1	9	6	4	4	5
Weight	20	8	7	4	2	4	5

Further, the interviewers were able to determine how the consumers were likely to use basic cutoff points when evaluating brands in certain ways, and these were also similar among the four interviewees.

Cutoff Points:

- Assume that a brand score of 4 or better on all attributes is required to surpass cutoff points for the Conjunctive model.

- Assume that a 5 or better on all attributes is required to surpass cutoff points for the Elimination-by-Aspects model.

Janet was very surprised to find that these four matching interviewees had subsequently participated in the very same focus group—the January 8, 2008, focus group (see previous case: "Decision Rules I: Introduction to Decision Rules"). The four matching interviewees were Laura M., Patricia L., Bruce F., and Doris A. She then decided to go back to the determinations she had made regarding the types of Decision Rules each of the focus group participants had used to see if these four had used different Decision Rules from one another. Finding that they had, she then used her knowledge of the different Decision Rules to make predictions regarding what choice of digital camera each consumer had made.

After she'd worked these predictions through, she was able to go back to the rebate forms that these consumers had sent in and see which camera they had actually purchased. She found that in all four cases, her prediction had been right on the money—a pretty good "hit rate" as far as she was concerned. She decided to print out all of this information and show it to the Trentron executives. She was hopeful that in presenting the data in this way, they would finally accept the importance of understanding the use of Decision Rules in consumers' decision-making processes.

Please do the following:

Using the table provided, as well as your answers to the case "Decision Rules I: Introduction to Decision Rules," to ascertain which brand of camera each of these four consumers (Laura M., Patricia L., Bruce F., and Doris A) likely purchased (where a compensatory Decision Rule was used, assume that this was a weighted compensatory rule). Please show all of your work (i.e., show each step in the decision process for each of the four consumers).

LAURA M	PATRICIA L	BRUCE F	DORIS A
EATTI = 5	LEX RULE	Comp Rule	CONJ RULE
PRINT QUALITY	PRINT QUALITY	BRAND A = 22	CTM = 4
BRAND A | BRAND D	BRAND A BRAND D	BRAND B = 37	
7 | 7	7 7	BRAND C = 30	BRANDS
PRICE = 2ND CRITERIA	PRICE = 2ND CRITERIA	BRAND D = 26	A, B, C, D
SELECTION	SELECTION	SELECTION	SELECTION
BRAND D = 10	BRAND D = 10	BRAND B	BRAND C

SECTION X:

QUALITATIVE AND INTERPRETIVE CONSUMER RESEARCH

30. Projective Techniques

Projective techniques are commonly used in the field of psychology. One of the most common of these is the Rorschach, or "Inkblot" test. This technique presents respondents with various meaningless shapes—the blots of ink. These shapes are completely ambiguous, because they have no meaning in and of themselves. Therefore, when respondents are asked to interpret the shapes, any meaning that they perceive is likely to be a projection of their own thoughts and feelings onto those shapes. Thus, the term "projective techniques."

These techniques have been used in marketing research contexts for many years. One of the earliest applications within marketing was conducted by Mason Haire in 1950.[1] After Nescafé brand of instant coffee was introduced to housewives in the 1940s, sales were disappointing. When directly questioned about the reasons behind their dislike of the product, housewives responded that they didn't like the taste. However, blind taste tests showed that taste was unlikely to be the real culprit, and led researchers to believe that there may be other reasons that housewives were reluctant to use the brand. Mason Haire, an MIT psychologist, was brought in to investigate the true reasons why housewives were not buying Nescafé instant coffee. Haire developed two shopping lists, and the only difference between the two was that one contained the Nescafé brand of instant coffee, and the other contained regular ground coffee. When housewives were shown one of the two shopping lists and asked to describe the person who had written the shopping list, the ones responding to the list containing instant coffee described a lazy and disorganized shopper, whereas the housewives responding to the list containing ground coffee described the shopper as good and sensible. As a result of this study, marketers of the Nescafé brand understood the true reluctance toward buying instant coffee, and could then address those issues directly.

The shopping lists in the above example are ambiguous in that they do not directly ask the respondent about her views on the subject of instant coffee. This practice of presenting an ambiguous stimulus and allowing the respondent to project his/her thoughts and feelings onto the ambiguous stimulus is a crucial aspect of all projective techniques.

Projective techniques are typically used in a one-on-one depth interview. They are often utilized when direct questioning has not been successful in uncovering some consumer insight and/or when it is thought that direct questioning will not reveal the true motivations, thoughts, and feelings that consumers possess. In those instances where consumers are *unable* and/or *unwilling* to share their real thoughts and feelings on a topic, projective techniques can be very effective.

Consumers are often *unable* to share their real thoughts and feelings on a topic because those thoughts and feelings are *implicit* rather than explicit. In other words, the thoughts and feelings are below the level of consciousness, making the consumer unaware of them. However, these unconscious thoughts and feelings can be extremely powerful in affecting attitudes and purchase decisions. In fact, some theorists have argued that in many cases, implicit knowledge may be

---

[1] Haire, M. (1950). "Projective Techniques in Marketing Research," *Journal of Marketing* , 649–656.

more important than explicit knowledge in influencing consumer behavior.[2] Projective techniques allow the researcher to delve below the level of consciousness to uncover these implicit thoughts and feelings.

When directly questioned, consumers are often *unwilling* to share their real thoughts and feelings on a topic because those thoughts and feelings are perceived as socially unacceptable, or consumers are uncomfortable expressing them because they view them as highly personal. In addition, many depth interviews utilizing direct questioning can be compromised by a certain amount of response bias—the respondents skew their answers to produce the responses that they believe the researcher wants to hear. Another reason that consumers may be unwilling to share their true thoughts and feelings may be culturally based. For example, in many Asian cultures it is thought to be somewhat rude to voice one's opinions directly, and in these cases, direct questioning will usually elicit no more than shallow and agreeable answers. By having consumers project their answers onto ambiguous stimuli (rather than take ownership of those thoughts and feelings themselves), projective techniques allow researchers to minimize consumers' social acceptability inhibition, desire to please the researchers, and unwillingness to share thoughts and feelings that they view as personal.

There are many different projective techniques that a marketer might utilize. We will discuss 10 specific techniques.

The first three have to do with completion tasks:

1. *Sentence Completion*—respondents are asked to complete a sentence stem.

2. *Story Completion*—respondents are asked to complete an unfinished story.

3. *Cartoon Completion*—respondents are asked to supply the caption for an unlabeled cartoon, or are asked to fill in an empty bubble that appears as a blank thought or comment balloon over the head or mouth of one of the characters in the cartoon.

The next three have to do with image creation and/or interpretation:

4. *Picture Sort*—respondents are asked to sort a series of pictures to reflect their association with different concepts. For instance, researchers may provide pictures of different people and ask respondents to sort them into piles by the type of car that they are likely to drive.

5. *Picture Interpretation*—This is similar to a Thematic Apperception Test (TAT) in psychology, where respondents are asked to tell a story about a picture that they are shown.

6. *Picture Drawing*—respondents are asked to draw a picture to reflect their thoughts and feelings on some topic.

---

[2] Please see: *Implicit Predictors of Consumer Behavior*, Harvard Business School, 9-502-043, prepared by Zaltman, G. & Puccinelli, N. M., Harvard Business School Publishing, 2002.

Others include:

7. *Word Association*—respondents are asked to quickly respond to a word that is presented by the researcher by saying the first thing that comes to mind.

8. *Third Person*—respondents are asked to describe what another person would feel, think, or do in a given situation.

9. *Typical User*—respondents are asked to describe the typical user of a product or service.

10. *Brand Analogies*—respondents are asked questions like, "If this brand were an animal, what type of animal would it be?" or "Imagine that this brand is a person—what would he/she be like? What might he/she say?" or respondents may even be asked to write a eulogy for a brand as if it had just died.

Often, two or more techniques can be combined and implemented as one. For example, researchers at McCann-Erickson, a large advertising agency, asked respondents to sketch typical buyers of two different brands of cake mixes: Pillsbury and Duncan Hines. They found that the Pillsbury user was pictured as plump and grandmotherly, and the Duncan Hines user was pictured as thin and contemporary.[3] This is an example of combining the Typical User technique with the Picture Drawing technique.

Whereas some research projects that utilize projective techniques are pure "fishing expeditions" with no real focus, most of these projects are conducted with some conjecture or hypothesis in mind. They use very pointed and precise techniques, and are looking for specific themes in the interviewees' responses.

The Scenario

Barbara Forrester is the marketing manager of the personal hygiene products division of a large conglomerate, O'Neill Products, Inc. O'Neill has been successful in many product categories, and this has been especially true in their personal hygiene products division; they are in the happy circumstance of being the market leader in almost every one of the product categories represented in this division. As market leader, O'Neill sometimes uses a marketing strategy that focuses on primary demand. In other words, because they are the market leader, they choose to concentrate on increasing demand throughout the product category, knowing that an increase in overall industry sales would benefit them to the greatest extent.

Barbara is meeting today with Jake Sullivan, who is the brand manager in charge of O'Neill's acne medication, Clearskin. For over a year now, Jake has been charged with the job of increasing sales to a specific segment of Clearskin's market—teenage boys. The project has not been going well. Whereas sales of some personal hygiene products to teenage boys have

---

[3] Miller, A., & Tsiantar, D. (1989, February 27). "Psyching Out Consumers," *Newsweek*, pp. 46–37.

increased dramatically over the last few years (for example, hair products), sales of acne medication to this segment have been stagnant. Barbara and Jake are meeting to discuss the results of some recent focus groups conducted to investigate teenage boys' thoughts and feelings regarding acne medications.

The Meeting

Barbara: "I've read through the focus group transcripts, and I have to say, there's not much here."

Jake: "I agree. I watched the focus group conducted here in town real-time, and I've watched the videos of the other two, and it's certainly hard to say anything definitive about teenage boys and acne medication based on these results. The moderator of the focus groups for Williams Marketing Research, Brian Grant, agrees with this as well. For some reason, the teenage boys seem unwilling or unable to articulate any meaningful opinions regarding this product category. Brian feels that although there are some underlying motivations regarding their avoidance of this product, the teens are either not completely conscious of these themselves, or are unwilling to share them with us."

Barbara: "Teenage boys are a notoriously difficult segment to read."

Jake: "A few months ago, we kicked around the idea of repackaging the product to appeal more to teenage boys. Some on the team also suggested renaming it; I know 'Zap-it!' was tossed around. The thinking was that this segment would be more likely to purchase a product that was made specifically for them, and that O'Neill would enjoy the benefits of being the first to market with this kind of a product."

Barbara: "I remember this line of thinking, and I want to keep that option open. However, I'm hesitant to spend the kind of money that this would require without having a specific strategy in place. To develop this strategy, we need to know more about this particular customer and his thoughts and motivations regarding the product."

Jake: "My early research showed that the numbers of teenage boys seeking treatment for acne from their physician matched the numbers for teenage girls. So we know that acne is as much of a problem for teenage boys as it is for teenage girls, and that they are motivated to take other steps to solve the problem. But when we asked the focus group participants why they didn't buy over-the-counter acne medications, a typical answer was "I don't buy that kind of thing.""

Barbara: "Oh, we know only too well that they don't buy that kind of thing! Now we need to find out *why* they don't. This might require a slightly different kind of research approach than the traditional methods we've been using. Why don't you meet with some of the Williams Research people and work out a plan for some motivation research using projective techniques. Try to get the focus group moderator to participate on this team if possible; I'd like to hear his thoughts. Work with them to put a proposal together, and have this to me within the next two weeks."

Please do the following:

Respond to the marketing manager's assignment by developing a proposal that utilizes any or all of the different types of projective techniques discussed in this case. Be specific and detailed regarding your research proposal. For example, if you suggest the use of word association, what *specific* words will you use? What *themes* will you be looking for in the answers?

Remember that the goal of this research is to *gain insight into the underlying reasons why teenage boys do not purchase acne medication.*

Many times, it helps to identify a hypothesis or two as you begin this type of research—these hypotheses are typically based on prior research and/or your "hunches" based on experience with these customers.

Therefore, your proposal should take the form:

A. Hypothesis/Hypotheses.

B. Projective Techniques Proposed (please utilize at least four different techniques from the list of projective techniques discussed in this case).

> PT 1: Describe *exactly how* you would use this technique, then describe what *themes/insights* you will be looking for in the respondents' answers.

> PT 2: Describe *exactly how* you would use this technique, then describe what *themes/insights* you will be looking for in the respondents' answers.

> PT 3: Describe *exactly how* you would use this technique, then describe what *themes/insights* you will be looking for in the respondents' answers.

> PT 4: Describe *exactly how* you would use this technique, then describe what *themes/insights* you will be looking for in the respondents' answers.

31. Laddering Interviews and Means-End Analysis

If you have taken a marketing course, you've heard the old adage, "Customers don't buy features; customers buy benefits." Some consumer behaviorists maintain that this is not the end of the story—that benefits are frequently not an end in themselves, but merely a means to achieving some valued end state that is important to the consumer. In other words, we might rewrite the adage to read: "Customers buy features that bring them benefits that get them closer to valued end states." These valued end states can be classified according to Kahle's List of Values (LOV):[1]

- Being Well Respected;
- Warm Relationships with Others;
- Fun and Enjoyment;
- Sense of Accomplishment;
- Self-Respect;
- Security;
- Excitement;
- Sense of Belonging; and
- Self-Fulfillment.

For instance, a customer might state that one of the reasons she bought a car is because it is red. When asked why the color red is important to her, she says that the color red is important to her because it means that the car is more likely to be noticed. So now we know something about one of the features (the color red) that is important to her, and her perception of the benefit that has been gained by that feature (being noticed). However, if we stopped the line of questioning here, we would not have a complete picture of this consumer's purchase motivations with regard to this feature. Note that at least two realistic possibilities exist with regard to the underlying reason that this benefit, "being noticed," is important to this consumer. If asked, "Why is being noticed important to you?" she might respond, "Because I like being noticed and admired by others." In this case, we would conclude that the benefit "being noticed" is important to this consumer because it leads to the valued end state of being well respected.

Feature	Benefit	Valued End State
color red ⟶	being noticed ⟶	being well respected

On the other hand, the consumer might respond that the benefit of "being noticed" is important to her "Because it means that other drivers are more likely to see the car, and therefore I am less likely to be in a car accident." In this case, we would conclude that the benefit "being noticed" is important to this consumer because it leads to the valued end state of security.

Feature	Benefit	Valued End State
color red ⟶	being noticed ⟶	security

---

[1] Kahle, L., & Kennedy, P. (1988, Fall). "Using the List of Values (LOV) to Understand Consumers," *Journal of Consumer Marketing*, 49–56.

Obviously these two different responses lead the consumer behaviorist to very different conclusions with regard to the consumer's purchase motivations.

The process that is used to identify the underlying links between features, benefits, and valued end states is called a "laddering interview," and consists primarily of repeatedly asking a consumer to identify why something is important to him/her—in fact, this questioning is repetitive to the extent that it typically feels awkward for both the interviewer and the respondent. However, this push to identify the underlying reasons that a consumer sees a feature or benefit as important is at the core of the laddering interview.

A very simplified hypothetical laddering interview follows:

Interviewer: "Why do you buy this particular yogurt?"

Consumer: "Well, the most important thing is that it's nonfat, but I also like that it's got calcium in it."

Interviewer: "Why is nonfat important?"

Consumer: "I'm on a diet, and being nonfat is important because it helps me to control my weight. But I don't like the taste as much as the full fat kind."

Interviewer: "Why is controlling your weight important to you?"

Consumer: "I think that when I control my weight other people respect me more."

Interviewer: "You said earlier that the fact that this yogurt is nonfat means that you don't like the taste as much as full fat yogurts. Why is this important to you?"

Consumer: "Well, I suppose because liking the taste leads to enjoyment, and enjoyment is important to me."

Interviewer: "Earlier you mentioned that one of the reasons that you purchase this yogurt is the calcium it contains. Why is this important to you?"

Consumer: "I've read that calcium can help fight osteoporosis."

Interviewer: "Why is this important to you?"

Consumer: "I want to feel secure that my bones are strong and won't break easily."

Interviewer: "Thank you very much for the interview."

Given the previous interview, the researcher would "map" what are called "Means-End Chains" to illustrate the relationships uncovered by the laddering interview. When all Means-End Chains are illustrated on the same map, that map is called a Hierarchical Value Map. Continuing the very simplified yogurt example, the means-end chains derived from the previous interview would likely appear in a Hierarchical Value Map as follows:

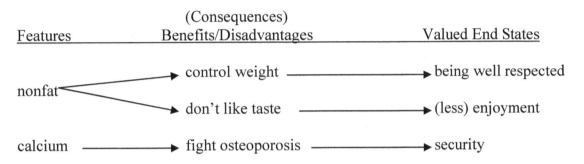

Features	(Consequences) Benefits/Disadvantages	Valued End States
nonfat	control weight	being well respected
	don't like taste	(less) enjoyment
calcium	fight osteoporosis	security

Notice that the interview, and therefore the map, may identify more than one product feature. In this particular case the map identifies two product features that are important to this consumer: nonfat and calcium. Note also that one feature may lead to more than one consequence, and that some consequences may be positive (or benefits), while others may be negative (or disadvantages), which in turn can lead to greater or lesser attainment of valued end states.

One of the most difficult aspects of mapping a laddering interview is making sure that each and every relationship is valid and an accurate representation of the statements made by the consumer. The arrows in the map represent clear, identifiable links between a feature and a consequence, or a consequence and a valued end state. Unless the link is readily apparent from the laddering interview, it should not be mapped—*these relationships should never be assumed by the interviewer.*

Part 1

Below you will find the transcript of a hypothetical laddering interview related to a new type of eating utensils. This new cutlery (knives, forks, spoons) is made from ceramic materials. A recent purchaser of this new cutlery was interviewed using the laddering technique.

Interviewer: "Why did you purchase this new type of cutlery?"

Consumer: "The main reason was because they are ceramic, but I also like the funky colors that they come in."

Interviewer: "Why is the fact that they are ceramic important to you?"

Consumer: "Because it means that I can put them in the microwave. Unfortunately, the fact that they are ceramic also means that they are more expensive than regular utensils."

	Interviewer:	"Why is being able to put them in the microwave important to you?"

| | Consumer: | "Because they won't cause the microwave to explode and hurt me!" |

Interviewer: "Why is being able to put them in the microwave important to you?"

Consumer: "Because they won't cause the microwave to explode and hurt me!"

Interviewer: "You said earlier that the fact that they are ceramic means that you have to pay more for them. Why is this important to you?"

Consumer: "It makes me feel badly about myself when I spend more than I know I should on something"

Interviewer: "You also said that you like the different colors that are available with these utensils. Why is this important to you?"

Consumer: "It keeps me in fashion."

Interviewer: "And why is being in fashion important to you?"

Consumer: "I feel like others look up to me when I stay in fashion"

Interviewer: "Any other reasons for choosing this product that you can think of?"

Consumer: "No—that's about it."

Interviewer: "Thanks very much for the interview."

Please create a Hierarchical Value Map below that contains the Means-End Chains representing the relationships uncovered by the previous laddering interview related to ceramic utensils. When articulating appropriate "valued end states," please choose from Kahle's List of Values (LOV).

	(Consequences)	
Features	Benefits/Disadvantages	Valued End States

Part 2

Those in the advertising profession employ these means-end chains and Hierarchical Value Maps through the use of a model known as the MECCAS (Means-End Conceptualization of the Components of Advertising Strategy) model.[2] The MECCAS model requires that the components of one of the identified means-end chains derived from a laddering interview are utilized in the development of an ad, such that:

- the valued end state identified by the consumer becomes the "driving force" of the ad, or the end goal that serves as a motivation for purchase;

- the product feature identified by the consumer becomes the "message element" of the ad or the brand attribute that is depicted in the ad;

- the benefit associated, by the consumer, with the brand attribute that is depicted in the ad becomes the "consumer benefit," or the major positive consequence of using the brand as depicted in the ad;

- the way in which the valued end state is associated with, or linked to, the identified brand attributes and/or the identified benefit are called the "leverage point(s)"; and

- the type/style of advertisement employed to communicate all of the above is called the "executional framework."

For instance, in the previous yogurt example, an advertiser would focus on the first means-end chain identified in the map (in this case, nonfat → control weight → being well respected). **Typically, advertisers focus on the means-end chain that has a positive result and that is the highest importance to the consumer.**

To continue the example, the yogurt ad might show two women eating yogurt; one is eating the advertised brand, which is nonfat, and the other is eating a competitor's brand, which is not nonfat. The ad then depicts these two women stepping on weight scales at home; the woman who ate the advertised brand has a big smile on her face while the one who ate the competitor's brand looks discouraged. The next scene shows the two women walking down a public street; the woman who ate the advertised brand of yogurt is receiving approving looks from bystanders, while the woman who ate the competitor's yogurt is not.

In this case, the parts of the MECCAS model would be:

- *Message Element(s):* nonfat feature
- *Consumer Benefit(s):* controlling weight
- *Driving Force:* being well respected

---

[2] Olson, J., & Reynolds, T. J. (1983). "Understanding Consumers' Cognitive Structures: Implications for Advertising Strategy." In L. Percy, & A. Woodside, *Advertising and Consumer Psychology.* Lexington, MA: Lexington Books, pp. 77–90.

- *Leverage Point(s):* the nonfat feature is linked to weight control benefit through the smile of the first woman when on the scale, and the weight control benefit is linked to the value of being well respected through the admiring looks of bystanders that only the first woman receives.
- *Executional Framework:* comparative advertisement

Please do the following:

Develop an ad utilizing the MECCAS model. The ad should be based on one of the means-end chains that you have identified as part of the Hierarchical Value Map that you created in Part 1 of this case (related to ceramic eating utensils). Please be careful to base your ad on *one* complete chain within the map (not a mixture of different chains from the same map). Be sure to describe the ad fully, and also be sure to identify the following *four* parts of the MECCAS model (as is done in the previous yogurt ad example): Message Element, Consumer Benefit, Driving Force, and Leverage Point(s). It is not necessary to identify the Executional Framework of the ad.

Description of ad (this ad may be print, broadcast, etc.—your choice):

Specifically identify these four parts of the ad that you have described above:
1. Driving Force—
2. Message Element—
3. Consumer Benefit—
4. Leverage Point(s)—

32. Information Display Boards

Ken barely made it to the airport in time to catch his flight home. As he boarded the plane, he realized that, once again, he hadn't seen any of the local attractions he had promised himself he would visit. This always seemed to be the case with these overseas business trips; he would work nonstop and never see the outside of the hotel. As he settled himself into his seat, he introduced himself to the person in the seat next to him.

The two travelers began to chat about their jobs, and Ken described his work: "I specialize in consumer research. I study people and their consumption behavior."

"Well, I wish you had seen me in the local drugstore a few days ago," said Steven, the corporate attorney seated next to Ken, "I was completely flummoxed, and all I was trying to do was buy some toothpaste! None of the brands I recognized were stocked there. I had to find someone in the store who knew a little English, and ask him to translate the information on the sides of the packages. It was a little embarrassing."

"Actually," said Ken, "That's a scenario I've used before in my work. I ask people to imagine that they are in a foreign country and need to buy a product like your toothpaste. There are no familiar brands, so they need to gather information on each of the unfamiliar brands from scratch.

"We do a lot of this type of research on the computer now—respondents are able to 'click' on certain parts of the screen to uncover information about each of the 'foreign' brands that we have presented to them. We ask test subjects to gather only the information they need to make a purchase decision, and stop when they have enough information to make that decision. We're very interested in the types of information that they gather and the order in which it is gathered. By studying these patterns, we learn a great deal about how consumers make purchase decisions in that product category, and the types and amount of information on which they base their purchase decisions.

"I'm in danger of sounding really old here," Ken continued, "But I remember a time when this was done with just a cardboard sheet and some papers covering up the brand information—before we used computers in the ways we do now. As a matter of fact, I can make an Information Display Board—that's what this particular research device is called—with the materials I've got in my briefcase: some paper and a few sticky notes. Feel like killing some time?"

"Sure," said Steven, "We've got hours stretched out in front of us, so why not?"

Ken put together a rudimentary Information Display Board for the product category toothpaste. When he finished, the paper looked like this:

Product Attributes	Brand A	Brand B	Brand C	Brand D
Gel vs. Paste				
Price				
Fluoride (yes/no)				
Flavor				

All of the attribute information for each brand was covered up by the small sticky notes. Ken instructed Steven to remove the sticky notes covering just those pieces of information that Steven wanted to know in order to decide which toothpaste to buy.

The first thing that Steven did was to remove all the sticky notes from the row labeled "Gel vs. Paste." Brand B was a gel, and Brands A, C, and D were paste. Then Steven removed the sticky notes covering the flavor information for Brands A, C, and D. Brand A was wintergreen, and Brands C and D were spearmint. Then Steven removed the price information for Brand C. The price was $2.25. Steven announced that he would buy Brand C. When he was finished with the Information Display Board, it looked like this:

Product Attributes	Brand A	Brand B	Brand C	Brand D
Gel vs. Paste	Paste	Gel	Paste	Paste
Price			$2.25	
Fluoride (yes/no)				
Flavor	Wintergreen		Spearmint	Spearmint

"Let's analyze your pattern of information collection," said Ken, "The first thing you did was gather information for every brand regarding whether the toothpaste was in gel or paste form. In most cases, the attribute that the consumer looks at first is the one that has the most importance for that consumer. So we'll assume that the gel vs. paste attribute is the most important to you when buying toothpaste."

"That's true," responded Steven, "I really don't like gel toothpastes, so it's important to me to stay away from them. Brand B was definitely out of the running when I saw that it was a gel."

"Right. Then you looked at the flavors of the paste brands. We'll assume flavor is your next most important attribute."

"Yeah, I was trying to match the flavor of my regular toothpaste, which is peppermint. When none of them were peppermint, I decided spearmint was closer than wintergreen."

"Next, you gathered information regarding the price of one of the two remaining paste/spearmint brands. After seeing this price, you had gathered enough information and decided to buy Brand C. The fact that you only looked at price information for one of the two contending brands—Brands C and D—rather than looking at the price information on both, tells me a lot."

"Well, toothpaste isn't very expensive," said Steven, "I didn't feel that I needed to spend time looking for the absolute best price. I just wanted to make sure that the price was within a reasonable range, and since Brand C's price was within what I consider a reasonable range, I didn't need to look any further."

"Exactly," said Ken, "We call this satisficing. You just wanted to make certain that a brand met some reasonable standard; you weren't looking for the 'best' with regard to that attribute. If you had looked at all the price information for the brands that had met the previous criteria, in this case Brands C and D, I would have assumed that you were trying to 'optimize' on that attribute, or in this case find the lowest price. But since you only checked the price of one of the two contending brands, we say that you are 'satisficing' on this attribute, or merely making sure that a reasonable standard is met on that attribute.

"I also noted," continued Ken, "That you didn't remove any of the sticky notes covering fluoride information. I can safely assume that this attribute holds no importance for you when purchasing toothpaste."

"You'd be right about that," answered Steven, "I have fluoride in my water at home, so it's completely irrelevant to me whether the toothpaste I buy contains fluoride or not."

"Okay, let's look at another possibility," said Ken as he replaced the sticky notes on the Information Display Board and then removed them in another pattern, "What if I first gathered information on price for all of the brands, then, finding that Brand B had the lowest price, uncovered information regarding whether Brand B had fluoride. Finding that Brand B contained fluoride, I say that I'm purchasing Brand B. What do you make of that?"

"I would say that price is the most important attribute for you, and your goal was to 'optimize' on that attribute by finding the lowest price," Steven said, "Fluoride was the next most important attribute for you, and you were looking for a toothpaste that contained fluoride. Since the lowest priced toothpaste did contain fluoride, that's the toothpaste you purchased. Whether the toothpaste was a gel or paste and the flavor of the toothpaste had no importance to you."

Ken smiled, "You've got the idea. These Information Display Boards aren't rocket science, but they can be a good way to gain insight into how consumers make decisions and the information that they base those decisions on."

Steven said, "This is great. Would you hand me the paper and sticky notes? I want to develop one of these things for the product category of laundry detergents—one of the products that my company makes. I'll try to find some unsuspecting traveler to take the 'test' for me, and I'll let you know what I find out."

Please do the following:

1. Create an Information Display Board for laundry detergents using four brands (call these Brands A, B, C, and D), and four product attributes: price, scent, liquid vs. powder, and the inclusion of a fabric softener (yes/no).

2. Find someone to use the Information Display Board in the way it is intended (you may want to set up a scenario much like the one described in paragraph four of this case).

3. *Record* and *interpret* their responses (the pattern they use to uncover information and what this means to you as an investigator of consumer behavior).

SECTION XI:

CULTURAL AND SUBCULTURAL INFLUENCES

33. The Diversity of Customer Behavior

Below you will find three requests for information, and each request requires you to answer for yourself and also to estimate how the other members of your class will answer (by estimating a class average and a class high and a class low). In other words, for each question, you should answer as accurately as possible for yourself, and then guess at what the class average and class high and low will be.

For now, ignore the second line (in italics) under each question; once all members have finished answering the three questions, an actual class average, a class high, and a class low for each question will be calculated.

1. Estimate the number of 12-oz. servings of carbonated beverage (soda pop) that you/your classmates consume per week.

You:_____ Class Average:_____ Class Low:_____ Class High:_____

(Actual Class Average:_____) (Actual Class High:_____) (Actual Class Low:_____)

2. Estimate the number of gifts for others that you/your classmates purchase in one year.

You:_____ Class Average:_____ Class Low:_____ Class High:_____

(Actual Class Average:_____) (Actual Class High:_____) (Actual Class Low:_____)

3. Estimate the number of ticketed (not free-of-charge) entertainment events (e.g., concerts, plays, comedy shows, exhibits, etc.) that you/your classmates attend in one year (do not include movies or sporting events in this estimate).

You:_____ Class Average:_____ Class Low:_____ Class High:_____

(Actual Class Average:_____) (Actual Class High:_____) (Actual Class Low:_____)

34. Culture and Customer Behavior

KKG, Inc., is an appliance and small electronics manufacturer in the United States that markets a wide variety of product lines. One of KKG's most successful new products in the past few years has been the Cook 'N Cool, a small, mobile appliance that is capable of both heating and cooling foods and liquids. Since the Cook 'N Cool has enjoyed a good deal of success domestically, senior management at KKG is now exploring the possibility of going international with the product. A traditional, comprehensive assessment of potential export countries has been undertaken, and the field of potential sites has been narrowed to three countries. Members of senior management have decided that they would like to begin slowly with the export of this product, and initially invest only enough funds to export to one country.

Sharon Bradley works in the market research area at KKG. Her boss, Jim Hayes, is one of the members of senior management. Jim has asked Sharon to take the three prospective export countries and rank them according to market potential for the Cook 'N Cool, and include in the report a clear and concise justification for this ranking. He stated that since the three potential export sites were nearly identical in terms of the traditional aspects of export analysis, he was counting on her to bring fresh insight to the problem. In other words, he was asking her to come up with a new way of analyzing the three potential countries that would "break the tie" between them. He asked her to work with Charlie Lowry, a new hire in the marketing area.

The Meetings

Sharon: "I have gone over and over the export analyses for these three countries, and it's almost eerie how similar they are in all aspects of traditional export analysis. On the other hand, I know that they are very different with regard to their cultures. But culture is a very abstract concept—it just can't be measured as easily as something like average disposable income, for example. And yet even though it can be difficult to measure, I believe that our answers lie with these three countries' very distinct cultures."

Charlie: "Were you on the team that did the initial analysis of the market potential for the product domestically? What did you find in that analysis?"

Sharon: "Well, I'm going back a few years, but I do remember that innovativeness was very closely tied to acceptance of the Cook 'N Cool. In other words, consumers who scored high on the innovativeness scale tended to be very excited about the Cook 'N Cool, and those who scored low had absolutely no use for it. A good deal of our domestic success with this product can be tied to our strategy to target highly innovative consumers."

Charlie: "I wonder if we could extrapolate those findings to the export arena, and argue that those cultures that tend to be high in innovativeness represent superior potential for this product than those cultures that tend to be low in innovativeness."

Sharon: "I think you're definitely headed in the right direction there. However, the three countries we're analyzing are not exactly mainstream export avenues. I'm doubtful that we'll be able to find any definitive information on the innovativeness of each of these cultures."

Charlie: "I'd be willing to devote the rest of the day to seeing what I could find with regard to that. I'm so new here that I don't have a lot of other projects going on. We could meet again tomorrow, and I'll let you know what I was able to find."

Sharon: "Alright—thanks. I'll see you tomorrow."

(They meet again the next day.)

Sharon: "Any luck?"

Charlie: "No—your doubts were right on target. There was nothing I could find that addressed anything about innovativeness within these three cultures. But while I was doing the search, I kept thinking about some cultural dimensions I studied in college. When I got home last night, I pulled out my old global business text to refresh my memory, and there they were: Hofstede's Cultural Dimensions.[1] Are you familiar with Hofstede's dimensions?"

Sharon: "Actually, no. I was an English major in college. Believe me, you don't even want to know the circuitous path that led me to this job. So tell me about these cultural dimensions."

Charlie: "Well, one of the reasons that I remember them so well is because of the way that my global business course was taught. I had two professors team-teaching the course—an anthropology professor and a business professor—and they disagreed vehemently over the usefulness of these dimensions. The anthropology professor felt strongly that these dimensions were almost useless because they were so general. She argued that they encouraged a broad and necessarily shallow understanding of a culture, whereas one could only truly appreciate the richness of a culture through comprehensive and detailed study. On the other hand, my business professor argued that the dimensions are useful precisely *because* they serve as generalizations. She argued that in the business world, we often don't have the time or resources to conduct comprehensive cultural studies. We must therefore rely on broad generalizations, however imperfect they may be. In effect, she was arguing that generalizations are better than no information at all. Anyway, Sharon, I've typed up a short summary of four of the most widely used of these cultural dimensions for you—I'm interested in seeing whether you believe they're useful in this particular situation. Take a look…"

---

[1] Hofstede, G. (1980). *Culture's Consequences*. Beverly Hills, CA: Sage.

Individualism vs. Collectivism—the value that members of a culture attach to their own personal advancement versus the advancement of the groups and institutions to which they belong.

Large vs. Small Power Distance—the degree to which a culture's members accept unequal power distribution and tend to be submissive to authority.

High vs. Low Uncertainty Avoidance—the degree to which members of a culture feel threatened by ambiguity and uncertainty.

Masculinity/Femininity—the degree to which gender roles are clearly defined, and one or the other set of traditional norms/values is seen as superior.

"I think we could argue that two of these dimensions are likely to be strongly correlated with consumer innovativeness: High vs. Low Uncertainty Avoidance, and Individualism vs. Collectivism."

Sharon: "I agree. And were you able to find information with regard to how our three potential export countries are rated with regard to these dimensions?"

Charlie: "Yes—thankfully, the use of these cultural dimensions is fairly widespread. I've created a table that summarizes how each of the three countries was rated on each of the four dimensions."

	Country A	**Country B**	**Country C**
Individualism vs. Collectivism	Indiv.	Collect.	Indiv.
Large vs. Small Power Distance	Large	Small	Large
High vs. Low Uncertainty Avoidance	High	High	Low
Masculinity/ Femininity	Masc.	Fem.	Masc.

Sharon: "You've really got something here, Charlie. This gives us a fresh new perspective. I have to say, I'm impressed with the creativity and resourcefulness you've shown in approaching this problem. How long do you think it will take to write this up? Remember that Jim asked for something clear and concise; it shouldn't run more than half a page."

Charlie: "I'll have it ready for you to review this afternoon."

Please do the following in a separate document:

Rank the countries in terms of market potential, and write a strong, reasoned argument supporting that ranking.

Do not assume that the readers of this document have any knowledge of the content of Sharon and Charlie's discussions. This document must stand alone; in other words, you will not be present to "fill in the blanks"—your reasoning must be clear to all who read the document. You may assume that Jim Hayes and other members of KKG's senior management have some rudimentary knowledge of Hofstede's dimensions.

Your argument should be clear and concise, and should not exceed half a page in length.

35. The Chinese Consumer

A 2005 *BusinessWeek* article advised businesspeople that learning about Chinese consumers should be "the No. 1 task for multinational and domestic (Chinese) companies alike."[1] Those are very strong words. Why all the attention?

Consider:

- The population of China now exceeds 1.3 billion, *four times* the population of the United States.[2]

- For the last quarter century, China's economy has grown around 9% per year, the fastest growth rate for a major economy in recorded history.[3]

- The emergence of China's middle class has been unprecedented, and continued further growth is expected.[4] China's political leaders placed the creation of a robust consumer economy at the heart of their most recent national five-year plan.[5]

The enormous market size and rapidly increasing purchase power of Chinese consumers pose tremendous opportunities and challenges for marketers. Exports to China are now among the crucial factors propelling growth for many countries, and most multinational companies' current and future success depends on an understanding of the Chinese consumer. Therein lies the challenge, for as KPMG reported a few years ago, "Chinese consumers have had more false assumptions made about them than almost anywhere else in the world."[6] We are slowly beginning to make progress in our understanding of the Chinese consumer. In a recent McKinsey & Co. survey of brand managers responsible for brands in China, 85% professed "some understanding but with 'a lot…that I still don't know.'" Only 7% stated that they had a good understanding of the Chinese consumer.[7]

Test your own knowledge of the Chinese consumer. Just by completing this quiz and checking your answers with those that the professor provides, you will be far ahead of your peers in the very important task of understanding the Chinese consumer. If you score higher than 50%, you have done very well.

---

[1] Roberts, D., & Rocks, D. (2005, October 17). "Let a Thousand Brands Bloom," *BusinessWeek*, pp. 58–60.
[2] Zakaria, F. (2005, May 9). Does the Future Belong to China? Newsweek.
[3] Zakaria, F. (2005, May 9). Does the Future Belong to China? Newsweek.
[4] Fang, B. (2006, May 1). "Spending Spree," *US News & World Report*.
[5] McGee, S. (2007, June 29). "Land of 1.3 Billion Shoppers," *MSN Money*.
[6] KPMG International. (2004). *Consumer Markets in China—The Real Deal?*
[7] St-Maurice, I., Sussmuth-Duckerhoff, C., & Tsai, H. (2008). "What's New with the Chinese Consumer," *McKinsey Quarterly*.

(Please note that the astronomical rate of change in China may mean that some of the statistics have changed. Where appropriate, an attempt has been made to include concurrent comparison statistics for other countries as reference points.)

_____ 1. The population of China is approximately _____ of the world's total population.
    a. one-fifth
    b. one-tenth
    c. half
    d. one-sixteenth

_____ 2. In the Unites States, a car costs the average consumer about 30%–40% of the consumer's annual income. In China, a car costs the average consumer about _____ of the consumer's annual income.
    a. 80%
    b. 20%
    c. 140%
    d. 1,000%

_____ 3. In terms of the global luxury goods market, Japan and the United States rank as the top two luxury goods markets. China ranks number _____ in the world regarding its luxury goods consumption.
    a. 10
    b. 25
    c. 82
    d. 3

_____ 4. Regarding the consumption/purchase process of the current average Chinese consumer,
    a. they purchase in a fashion very similar to their grandparents and great-grandparents; same types of products and purchase processes.
    b. they are very savvy, with a strong history as consumers.
    c. they feel very new to the consumption process, and are looking for guidance in many product categories.
    d. they hate to shop and so avoid the purchase process whenever possible.

_____ 5. Regarding a Wal-Mart superstore in China, choose the following statement that is FALSE.
    a. Most foods must be frozen, rather than fresh, since Chinese shoppers only shop about two times per month.
    b. The fish section of the store has more fish tanks than display counters, and a small net is provided to shoppers so that they can choose their live fish.
    c. There is a tea tasting section, so that shoppers can sample a tea before buying.
    d. Shoppers might ride the Wal-Mart shuttle to their homes after making their purchases.

_____ 6. A trendy status symbol for upscale Chinese consumers is
  a. red wine (rather than the traditional rice wine).
  b. pet dogs.
  c. golf/country clubs.
  d. all of the above.

_____ 7. Regarding the Chinese consumers' attitudes toward domestic brands vs. foreign brands in most product categories,
  a. Chinese consumers are proud of homegrown brands and have typically favored Chinese brands over foreign brands, all else being equal.
  b. Chinese consumers have typically favored foreign brands over Chinese brands.
  c. Chinese consumers typically do not have a choice of brands, since only one brand is available in most product categories.

_____ 8. Regarding Starbucks in China,
  a. there are very few Starbucks in China, and the few that are there have a 3-day waiting period to get in.
  b. there are many Starbucks in China, and they are most crowded in the morning, as the Chinese fight for their morning coffee.
  c. there are many Starbucks in China, and they are most crowded in the evening, since Starbucks is seen as a place to gather and socialize.
  d. there are no Starbucks in China.

_____ 9. Around 60% of Chinese families own their own home, a surprisingly high number. Of those, _____ paid cash for their home.
  a. 100%
  b. 83%
  c. 17%
  d. 32%

_____ 10. The most popular attire for a Chinese bride is a(n):
  a. traditional red embroidered silk wedding gown.
  b. Western-style white wedding gown.
  c. upscale business suit.
  d. most weddings are very simple; the bride does not "dress up."

_____ 11. Chinese consumers tend to be pro-American, and this is at least in part because of historical Chinese-American relations. They tend to think well of America's role in their country because:
  a. the United States was not involved in the early 20th-century imperialism of concessions granted to the French, British, and Russians.
  b. the United States was a Chinese ally in World War II.
  c. the United States fought against Japanese occupation in China during the 1940s.
  d. all of the above.
  e. none of the above; the Chinese consumer is decidedly NOT pro-American.

_____ 12. A well-respected expert on the Chinese consumer proposes that a modern Chinese woman enhances her physical beauty primarily to
    a. attract a husband, upon whom she will be financially dependent.
    b. get ahead in her career.
    c. impress other women.
    d. please her parents, who have invested a great deal in her.

_____ 13. In 2007, Europe boasted 36 cities with over 1 million residents. The United States had 9 cities with over 1 million residents. China had _____ cities with over 1 million residents.
    a. 5
    b. 150
    c. 25
    d. 500

_____ 14. About 70% of middle-class Chinese families send their children over the age of three to at least one for-profit extra-curricular class outside of normal school hours. Of the following, the most popularly chosen class is:
    a. math.
    b. English.
    c. physics.
    d. chemistry.

_____ 15. A few years ago, McKinsey & Co. investigated Chinese consumers' attitudes and values. Which of the following phrases did the average Chinese consumer choose as being "closest to own attitude"?
    a. Work hard and get rich.
    b. Don't think of money/fame; live a life that suits my own taste.
    c. Never think of self; give in service to society.
    d. a and c above were tied with 45% each.

_____ 16. In the above noted McKinsey & Co. investigation, which of the following phrases did 18- to 24-year-olds residing in large Chinese cities choose as being "closest to own attitude"?
    a. Work hard and get rich.
    b. Don't think of money/fame; live a life that suits my own taste.
    c. Never think of self; give in service to society.
    d. a. and c. above were tied with 45% each.

_____ 17. In 2007, US Global Investors reported that around 60% of middle-class Americans owned a personal computer. For the middle class Chinese, that number was
    a. 65%.
    b. 20%.
    c. 10%.
    d. 90%.

_____ 18. Young (18- to 25-year-old) Chinese consumers view the use of the Internet primarily as a way to

   a. gather information and get ahead in their jobs/school.
   b. engage in political debates.
   c. have fun/play games.
   d. connect with distant family members.

_____ 19. Chinese consumers typically view grocery shopping as

   a. a duty to fulfill for the good of the family.
   b. drudgery; if possible, they avoid it.
   c. something to be done quickly; convenience stores are very popular.
   d. entertainment; they love a vibrant and interactive atmosphere.

_____ 20. Chinese consumers rank among the world's _____ when it comes to understanding the importance of good nutrition

   a. highest
   b. lowest
   c. somewhere in the middle

_____ 21. When looking at the percentage of the national workforce that is female, the comparison between the United States and China reveals that

   a. the percentage of the workforce that is female is higher in China than in the United States.
   b. the percentage of the workforce that is female is higher in the United States than in China.
   c. they are roughly equivalent.

_____ 22. Of the following automobile brands, the one that, in 2008, the Chinese consumer most closely associated with status and success is

   a. Buick (GM).
   b. Lexus (Toyota).
   c. Acura (Honda).
   d. Volkswagen.

_____ 23. When comparing a supermarket in a big urban area in China with its counterpart in the United States, the number of brands that are available in a typical product category in China as compared to the number of brands available in the United States is as follows:

   a. the number of brands available in China is about double those available in the United States.
   b. the number of brands available in the United States is about double those available in China.
   c. the number of brands is slightly higher in China.
   d. the number of brands is slightly higher in the United States.
   e. the number of brands is roughly equal across the two countries.

_____ 24. Of the following product categories, the product category that received the *most* agreement with the statement "I prefer to buy domestic (rather than foreign) products" by Chinese consumers in 2007 was

    a. home appliances.
    b. high tech.
    c. consumer goods.
    d. financial services.
    e. apparel.

_____ 25. Of the following product categories, the product category that received the *least* agreement with the statement "I prefer to buy domestic (rather than foreign) products" by Chinese consumers in 2007 was

    a. home appliances.
    b. high tech.
    c. consumer goods.
    d. financial services.
    e. apparel.

_____ 26. In studying young Chinese consumers' attitudes toward the future, researchers find that they are overwhelmingly _____

    a. depressed; the pressure of being an only child (due to China's "one-child policy") has placed enormous burdens on these young people.
    b. optimistic; they are confident in their abilities to be successful.
    c. worried; they are very aware of how competitive and difficult it is to get ahead in such a large and turbulent economy.

_____ 27. Of the following sources of product/service information, the source that is relied on most heavily by Chinese consumers is

    a. multimedia kiosks.
    b. Internet ads.
    c. TV ads.
    d. word of mouth.

_____ 28. Of the following sources of product/service information, which is used more heavily by Chinese consumers than their counterparts in the United States, France, Germany, Japan, and Korea?

    a. Multimedia kiosks
    b. Internet ads
    c. TV ads
    d. Word of mouth
    e. All of the above

_____ 29. A survey of top Chinese businesspeople revealed that they consider one country in the global economy to be their closest competitor. That country is
    a. the United States.
    b. Japan.
    c. India.
    d. Australia.

_____ 30. Approximately ___ of the Chinese population is literate (can read and write).
    a. 91%
    b. 82%
    c. 50%
    d. less than 50%

_____ 31. In China, the most common way to pay for purchases is
    a. a debit card.
    b. a credit card.
    c. cash.
    d. personal check.

_____ 32. Salesperson influence in the purchase process of the middle-class Chinese consumer is typically _____ than in other countries.
    a. higher
    b. lower
    c. about the same when comparing Chinese consumers with consumers in other countries

_____ 33. In a survey related to consumer values, approximately what percentage of Chinese consumers agreed with the statement "Stability is more important than excitement"?
    a. 20%
    b. 40%
    c. 65%
    d. 90%

_____ 34. What foreign brand is most often mistaken for a domestic (Chinese) brand by Chinese consumers?
    a. Crest
    b. Samsung
    c. Sony
    d. none; Chinese consumers are very knowledgeable about country-of-origin issues

_____ 35. In 2007, 41 brand managers responsible for brands in China were asked to prioritize market segments with regard to the importance of developing an understanding of that consumer group. The Chinese consumer groups/segments included teens, untapped rural consumers, wealthy consumers, and the rising urban middle class. Their first priority was:

a. teens.
b. untapped rural consumers.
c. wealthy consumers.
d. the rising urban middle class.

_____ 36. Regarding their financial futures, about _____ of Chinese adults agreed with the statement "I expect my child to support me when I get old" and about _____ of Chinese teens agreed with the statement "I will support my parents when they get old."

a. 95%; 75%
b. 95%; 25%
c. 80%; 95%
d. 95%; 80%

_____ 37. A 2008 survey showed that 21% of Americans viewed environmental friendliness as a key buying factor when purchasing a washing machine. The same survey showed that _____ of Chinese consumers viewed environmental friendliness as a key buying factor when purchasing a washing machine.

a. 2%
b. 27%
c. 0%
d. 45%

_____ 38. A well-respected expert on the Chinese consumer maintains that the two advertising themes that most resonate with Chinese consumers are

a. excitement and power.
b. serenity and pragmatism.
c. protection and escape.

_____ 39. The students who tend to be admired by their peers, and are therefore trendsetters in Chinese secondary schools, are typically the ones who

a. get good grades in school and please their parents.
b. are the most athletic.
c. are fashion risk-takers.
d. rebel against parental pressure to succeed.

_____ 40. In 2008, 52% of U.S. consumers and 43% of Japanese consumers listed an emotional factor (as opposed to more functional/pragmatic factors) as being *at least one* of their "top three" key buying factors when purchasing consumer electronics. In that same survey, _____ of Chinese consumers listed at least one emotional factor.

a. 6%
b. 80%
c. 68%
d. 29%

_____ 41. The Chinese population is moving from rural areas to cities in record numbers. The McKinsey Global Institute on Urbanization in China has estimated that by the year 2030, more than 1 billion Chinese will live in cities, and they will account for approximately _____ of total national consumption

a. 25%
b. 90%
c. 33%
d. 50%

_____ 42. Since 2006, U.S. consumers' average annual personal savings rate has dipped into the negative range. In other words, in many cases American consumers are actually spending more each year than they earn. The average annual personal savings rate for Chinese consumers is around

a. 15%–20%.
b. around 0 or slightly negative, similar to the United States.
c. 5%–7%.
d. 30%–33%.

_____ 43. The leading hypermarket/superstore supermarket chain in China is

a. Wal-Mart (US)
b. Carrefour (France)
c. Tesco (UK)
d. Lianhua (China)

_____ 44. Of the following, the source of product/service information that average Chinese consumers deem most important when considering *new products* is

a. newspaper advertisement.
b. TV advertisement.
c. magazine advertisement.
d. in-store information and promotions.

_____ 45. The typical upscale Chinese consumer replaces his/her cell (mobile) phone every

a. 2 years.
b. 5 years.
c. 1 year.
d. 3–6 months.

_____ 46. Approximately _____ of the world's cell (mobile) phones are in use in China.
   a. one-eighth
   b. one-twentieth
   c. one-half
   d. cell phone technology has not yet reached China

_____ 47. An average Chinese consumer can look forward to a retirement that includes
   a. full health care coverage, but no significant social security payments.
   b. full health care coverage and significant social security payments until death.
   c. no health care coverage but significant social security payments.
   d. neither health care coverage nor significant social security payments.

_____ 48. Typical middle-class Chinese consumers purchase high-priced goods
   a. for private use in the home; many consumers have experienced poverty, and now feel that they "deserve" to be pampered in private, but they must be humble in public and so they try not to "show off" with flashy goods.
   b. for public consumption; they see products as symbols of status, and tend to buy high-priced items for use in public, but downscale items for their private use.
   c. for both private and public consumption.
   d. for neither private nor public use; the typical middle-class Chinese consumer does not have the funds to purchase any high-priced items.

_____ 49. Japanese Internet users spend about 14 hours per week on the Internet. American Internet users spend about 12 hours per week on the Internet. Chinese Internet users spend about ____ hours per week on the Internet.
   a. 5
   b. 9
   c. 14
   d. 17

_____ 50. It took Blizzard Entertainment one year to sign up 1 million North American paying subscribers for its World of Warcraft™, a popular online game. In China, they signed up 1.5 million players in
   a. one year.
   b. one month.
   c. three years.
   d. they have not yet signed up 1.5 million players in China.